the handmade candle

alison jenkins

photography by emma peios

For Dave

The mission of Storey Communications is to serve our customers by publishing practical information that encourages independence in harmony with the environment.

North American edition published in 2001 by Storey Books,
Schoolhouse Road, Pownal, Vermont 05261
United Kingdom edition published in 2001 by New Holland Publishers (UK) Ltd,
24 Nutford Place, London W1H 6DQ

ISBN 1-58017-353-5

Editors: Christine Rista and Claire Waite
Production Controller: Caroline Hansell
Photographer: Emma Peios
Designer: Roger Daniels
Editorial Direction: Rosemary Wilkinson

10 9 8 7 6 5 4 3 2 1

Reproduced by Modern Age Repro House Ltd, Hong Kong
Printed and bound in Singapore by Tien Wah Press (Pte) Ltd

Important: The author and publishers have made every effort to ensure that all instructions given in this book are safe and accurate. They cannot accept liability for any resulting injury or loss or damage to either property or person, whether direct or consequential and howsoever arising. To give you the option of working in either ounces or grams, it has been necessary to round up or down the conversion figure slightly. These small differences will not affect your end result. Use either ounces or grams, but do not mix the two.

Credits: Many thanks to Senses Candle Design for the instructions and candles on page 62 and to David Constable for making the candles on pages 28, 38, 44, 58, 64, 66, 68, and 70.

contents

Candlemaking is a relatively simple craft with its origins firmly grounded in ancient history. The necessary materials and equipment are readily available from craft and specialty shops everywhere; in fact, you will probably find that you already possess most of the basic equipment in your kitchen at home. So, armed with this book, there is nothing to stop you from exploring this creative and satisfying craft.

Candlemaking requires a heat source; therefore, the obvious place to make candles is in the kitchen. But take heed: The craft is quite addictive and absorbing, as my poor parents will confirm. They paid me a brief visit while I was in the middle of the experimentation with and preparation of the projects in this book. My kitchen was strictly a candles only, no-cook zone, with hubbling, bubbling pans of molten wax on the stove and projects in various stages of completion balanced precariously on every available surface. "Let's go out for dinner," they suggested hopefully, with absolutely no arguments from me.

This book falls basically into two parts. You will find an information and techniques section, followed by a series of 21 inspirational projects. The first section provides comprehensive, illustrated details on the basic and more specialized equipment and materials you are likely to need, detailing the use and application of each.

introd

The basic techniques of candlemaking and some special effects are also described. By reading carefully through this section you will be able to confidently complete all the projects that follow.

It is by no means necessary to gather all the equipment at once. Instead it is advisable, if you are a complete beginner, to buy simply the bare essentials. Then, if the candlemaking bug bites, you can think about buying more expensive and varied materials and molds.

The projects chosen for this book are intended to both instruct and inspire and are designed as a practical starting point for candlemaking. Why not try your own combination of techniques and colors for spectacular effects? And don't forget, wax can always be remelted and reused, so don't despair if your early attempts are somewhat disappointing.

The joy of any new craft is being able to use basic, newfound skills together with your imagination and artistic style to create unique projects that are both useful and decorative and reflect a part of you. I am sure you will discover, as I have, that candlemaking is a wonderful and enjoyable way to express your own individuality and is also far more satisfying than buying ready-made, mass-produced candles from a store. I hope you will enjoy this book and will continue to enjoy making and using candles as a part of your life.

a brief history of candlemaking

How fortunate we are today to be able to illuminate darkness with the mere flick of a switch. The luxury of instant, artificial light, however, is a fairly recent one. No more than 150 years ago the humble candle and oil lamps were the only source of artificial light available. And yet, even though electricity and gas are now the common power sources in most homes, we still choose to use candles, no longer out of necessity but for the sheer irresistible charm of a flickering flame.

The basic methods of candlemaking remain the same as in centuries past. A candle is essentially a cylinder of solid fuel with a central wick. Traditionally, most candles for domestic use were made out of tallow, a substance obtained from animal fat, and wicks were made from rush or flax. However, tallow would smell revolting when burning, and rush or flax wicks smoked terribly. The only alternative material available for candlemaking was beeswax, which, because of its costliness, was reserved for use by the very wealthy and the church. And even then, because of the quality of the wicks, the candles often did not burn evenly.

In the early nineteenth century, because of the research and experimentation of a French chemist named Michael Chevreul, it was discovered that a substance called stearin could be separated from tallow. Stearin could be used to harden other fats, giving rise to the production of cheaper, odor-free, better-quality candles. As the century progressed, petroleum oil and coal were used increasingly as energy sources. A by-product of this industry was the extraction of paraffin wax.

These two basic ingredients, stearin and paraffin wax, transformed the burning quality of candles and, with the exception of beeswax, replaced all other substances used in the candlemaking process. They remain the principal

ingredients today, though stearin is now made from palm nuts, and paraffin wax is a by-product of refining gasoline.

Another great advance, which took place during the same period, was the introduction of braided wicks. Rush and flax wicks caused candles to burn unevenly and smoke and made it necessary to snuff and trim the wick at regular intervals. In 1825, another Frenchman, M. Cambaceres, experimented with different materials and produced a wick made from braided cotton threads, which was found to give a brighter, more constant flame. There still remained, however, the problem of the ash that was produced by the braided cotton. It was eventually

discovered that if wicks were soaked in boric acid they became self-consuming when lit. Coincidentally, it was just as candlemaking was finally perfected that the use of electricity as a source of lighting became viable and widespread.

Today, the use of candles is enjoying a revival, and candlemakers have access to a vast array of wax products, molds, and decorative materials with which to experiment. The projects in this book employ a range of simple techniques, which, I hope, will instruct and inspire you to create beautiful, original candles to keep for pleasure or to give as gifts.

necessities

Candlemaking techniques require a number of pieces of necessary equipment, some of which you probably have in your kitchen or home office. For the majority of projects described in this book, you will need a double boiler, a thermometer, a wicking needle, a suitable wick support, a craft knife, a cookie sheet, a water bath, weights, a mold, and a mold sealer. Any additional equipment is specified in the individual projects.

ADHESIVE TAPES: Double-sided adhesive tape is used in the construction of cardboard molds that are then sealed on the outside with packing tape. Strips of masking tape are used to mark the level to which a mold should be filled when you are making striped candles.

BRADAWL: This tool is used to pierce a hole in a "found" mold to thread the wick through.

CARDBOARD AND CARDBOARD TUBES: Sheets of stiff cardboard are useful for making candle molds, especially shiny cardboard that does not stick to wax. Ready-made cardboard tubes can also be used as pillar molds. Food containers can be easily adapted into candle molds.

COOKIE SHEET: It is often a good idea to put candle molds on a cookie sheet to catch any wax leakage, and then seal them in place with mold sealer.

CRAFT KNIFE: A sharp craft knife is an invaluable tool for the candlemaker in a multitude of ways, including its uses for simple wick trimming, cutting beeswax sheets to size, and cutting cardboard molds from templates.

DIPPING CAN: A tall, metal, cylindrical vessel is necessary for holding molten wax when making long, hand-dipped candles, and for the crackled pyramid

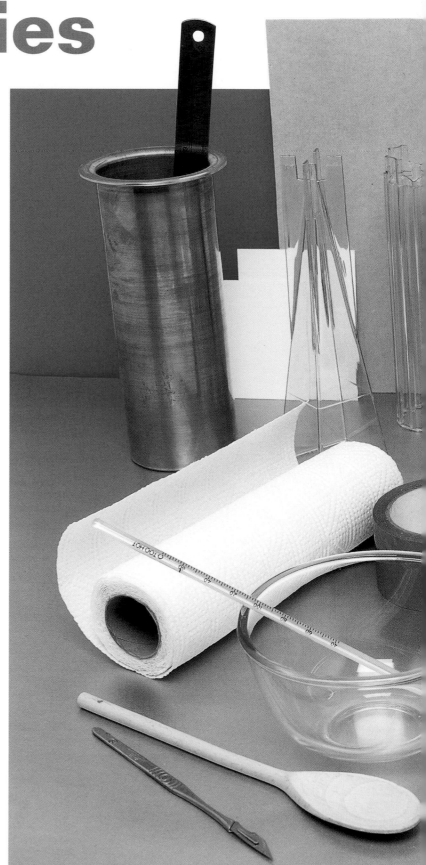

project (see pages 46–47). Dipping cans are available in a variety of sizes, depending on the size of the candle required. As they are a specialized and costly piece of equipment, you could use a tall metal food can instead.

DOUBLE BOILER: The double boiler, an essential piece of equipment in candlemaking, should be made from either aluminum or stainless steel. Wax begins to vaporize when it overheats and can then easily catch fire; therefore, the safest way to heat it is over water. Put the wax in the upper pan and water in the lower one. Then bring the water to a boil and leave it to simmer while the wax melts. Care must be taken not to let the lower pan boil dry, so remember to refill it regularly.

EMBOSSING MOLDS: Small, plastic decorative moldings can be bought to emboss candles. They are glued to the inside of cardboard molds using waterproof glue. Alternatively, you can cut out your own shapes from stiff cardboard and use them in the same way.

GLASS BOWLS: It is always advisable to have a few small glass containers close at hand for weighing wax, using as water baths, or storing small amounts of leftover wax for use at a later date.

HEAT SOURCE: Candlemaking is a craft that can be carried out in the kitchen using a gas or an electric stove. However, a small camping stove is useful if you have a separate workshop.

HEAVY WAXED PAPER: This paper is useful for lining glass containers used to hold leftover wax. It can also be dipped into stearin or wax so that you can check the approximate finished shade.

METAL SKEWER: A metal skewer is a useful implement for stirring molten wax or stearin, and it can be wiped clean with a paper towel. Do not leave the skewer in the hot mixture, and wear oven gloves to protect your hands.

MOLDS: There are a number of ready-made molds available to buy (see page 14), or you can make your own using cardboard or clean, "found" hollow objects, such as plastic or cardboard food containers, glass jars, or salad bowls (see pages 20–21).

MOLD SEALER: This candlemaking product is a sticky, puttylike, nonsetting pasty material that is waterproof and reusable. It is primarily used to seal around the wick and wick hole of a mold to prevent wax from leaking out. It can also be used to fix the base of cardboard molds to the cookie sheet, again to prevent wax seepage. The importance of using a good mold sealer cannot be stressed enough.

PAPER TOWELS: No candlemaker should be without a roll of paper towels within easy reach to mop up spills, clean thermometers, protect molds, and generally keep the work area clean.

PLAIN PAPER: Sheets of plain paper are useful to have around for tracing templates.

RULER: A metal ruler can be used to shape a candle made from rolled beeswax sheets and is also useful for scoring lines to help fold a cardboard mold.

SPOON: A wooden or metal spoon is useful for mixing wax, stearin, and dyes together in the double boiler. Wax dye should be crushed with the back of a metal spoon before it is added to molten stearin or wax.

THERMOMETER: Temperature control is a crucial element of the candlemaking process, as the quality and nature of the finished product often depend on pouring at just the right moment. The thermometer should be able to measure temperatures between 100°F (38°C) and 250°F (121°C). Always wipe it clean with a paper towel when you remove it from the wax. You could use a special wax thermometer from candlemaking suppliers or a sugar thermometer.

TRACING PAPER: Keep this transparent paper handy when making your own molds using the templates in this book (see pages 76–77).

WATER BATH AND WEIGHTS: Any container in which the mold can sit and be surrounded by water can be used as a water bath to shorten the wax setting time. Old-fashioned kitchen weights or pebbles can be used to hold down a rigid mold.

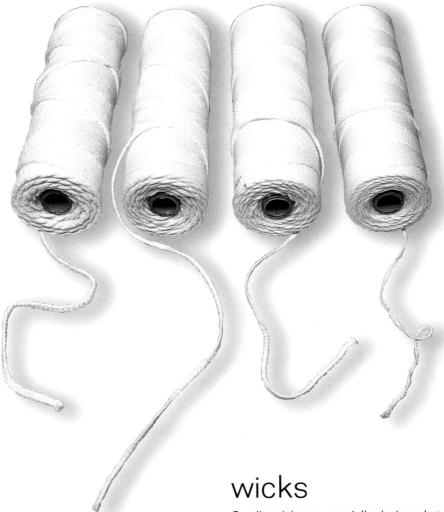

wicks

Candle wicks are specially designed strings of braided cotton treated with boric acid. They are available in various thicknesses to use with candles of different diameters and widths. It is extremely important to choose the correct size wick for each candle. If the wick is too large, it will provide too much heat, and the candle may smoke and wax may drip down the sides. On the other hand, if the wick is too small, it will burn down in a cavity in the center of the candle, causing the candle flame to become drowned in molten wax.

Professional candlemakers classify a wick by the number of strands it contains but, as the size of the wick is determined by the diameter or width of the candle you are making, most people simply ask their suppliers for this measurement. For example, for a 2 in (5 cm) candle you would need a 2 in (5 cm) wick. This will burn with a pool of wax that reaches just to the outside of the candle.

WICK SUPPORTS: Wooden cocktail sticks or skewers can be used to keep wicks vertical and centrally positioned in the mold while the molten wax is poured into it. The wick end is simply threaded onto or tied around the stick, which then rests across the shoulder of the mold, keeping the wick upright.

WICK SUSTAINERS: These small metal discs with a hole in the center are used to anchor the wick to the base of a mold that does not have a hole in it, such as a glass jar. Simply push the wick through the center of the sustainer and pinch the metal to hold the wick securely in place.

WICKING NEEDLE: These sturdy needles are used for threading wicks into molds and piercing holes in cardboard molds. They are available in a variety of sizes.

waxes

Wax, of course, is the main ingredient used in candlemaking, and there are two main types used for most candlemaking processes: paraffin wax and beeswax. Each has different qualities and is used in different ways or combinations to suit the project at hand. Paraffin wax, however, remains the most popular, as it is relatively inexpensive, readily available, and easily dyed any color, shade, or tint. There are also a number of special waxes available that can be used as additives and to make decorative effects.

APPLIQUÉ WAX: As the name suggests, appliqué wax, which comes in very thin sheets that are easily cut into shapes with a craft knife, is used for achieving applied decorative effects. The beauty of this wax is that it can be pressed onto the surface of a candle without the use of glue. Appliqué wax is available in various colors and metallic finishes and can also be bought in the shapes of letters and numbers.

BEESWAX: A more expensive alternative to paraffin wax, beeswax is a natural product with a delicious, honey fragrance. It is available in block form or in sheets that have a honeycomb pattern imprinted on the surface. The blocks are melted and molded just like paraffin wax, whereas the sheets are used for making rolled candles. At room temperature, beeswax sheets are soft, pliable, and extremely easy to work with. In its natural form, beeswax has a brownish color, but it is also available bleached white and in a range of dyed colors.

COMMERCIALLY PREPARED PARAFFIN WAX: Paraffin wax pellets can be obtained predyed with the correct amount of stearin and color already added. They can be mixed together to form other colors or used with uncolored wax to obtain lighter shades.

JELLY WAX: Jelly wax is a relatively new product and looks just like jelly, as the name suggests. It does not set hard like an ordinary wax. Therefore, it cannot be cast in a mold but instead must be poured into a container of some sort, preferably one made of glass.

MICRO WAXES: These waxes are added in varying proportions to paraffin wax to alter its setting time. Micro soft is added to allow the wax mixture to stay soft and malleable longer, which is useful for modeling projects. Micro hard is very hard and brittle when it is solid, and it has a higher melting point than paraffin wax does. It is used in the proportion of 1 percent with paraffin wax to strengthen candles and make them slower burning.

MOLDABLE WAX: This soft wax is available in small, predyed quantities that can be molded by hand or stamped with cookie cutters to make small or floating candles. It is particularly easy for children to use.

PARAFFIN WAX: This is the basic ingredient required for most candlemaking techniques. A by-product of the refining process of crude oil, paraffin wax is a translucent, odorless, tasteless substance. It is available in pellet form, which is very easy to use, or in slabs, which need to be cut into smaller pieces before they can be used. At room temperature, paraffin wax is solid, and it has a range of melting temperatures from 104 to 160°F (40 to 71°C). When it melts, it becomes colorless liquid; when it is removed from the heat source, it begins to solidify very quickly. In this semisolid state, it is easy to cut, mold, and embed objects into its surface to create various decorative effects.

STEARIN: This substance is often added to paraffin wax in a ratio of one part stearin to nine parts wax. It improves the burning quality and opacity of the candle and acts as a releasing agent when rigid molds are used.

WAX GLUE: This is wax in a very sticky form. A small amount is melted in a double boiler and used to stick any form of decoration to the surface of a candle.

ready-made molds

Ready-made candle molds are now available in a huge variety of shapes and sizes. Rigid molds are made from plastic, glass, or metal and are generally free-standing or, in the case of conical or pyramid shapes, are supplied with a small support. Flexible molds are made from latex and need to be supported with cardboard (see page 19).

CLEAR PLASTIC MOLDS: These are the molds most commonly used in this book. Clear plastic molds are strong and cheap; since they are transparent, they are useful when making multicolored, layered, or special-effect candles. Spherical or egg-shaped candles can be made in two-part molds. When you use plastic molds, the wax should be heated no higher than 180°F (82°C).

FLEXIBLE MOLDS: These molds are produced in a variety of shapes and sizes. Since they are made from a flexible material (latex), they can be produced in very intricate, irregular shapes with undercuts and deep reliefs. They do stretch and deteriorate over time, and they are difficult to hold when they are full of hot wax. Use wax at a temperature of 200°F (93°C) in flexible molds.

GLASS MOLDS: These produce high-gloss candles but are rather fragile and are limited to cylindrical shapes. Wax should be at a temperature of 180°F (82°C) when poured into glass molds.

METAL MOLDS: Metal molds are more expensive than their plastic counterparts but are longer lasting and more durable and have an excellent cooling rate. Wax at temperatures up to 195°F (90°C) can be poured into them.

MOLD-MAKING KIT: You can also make your own flexible latex molds using a special kit available from candlemaking suppliers. This consists of a latex solution and a thickener that can be painted over a three-dimensional shape, such as a piece of fruit or a pebble, to make an individually shaped mold. Always follow the manufacturer's instructions when making flexible latex molds. Wax is poured into these molds at a temp-erature of 200°F (93°C).

additions

You can add colors and scents to your handmade candles to make them truly individual and personal. Some of the projects in this book also show you how to add three-dimensional objects to your candles, such as seashells, glass nuggets, and mosaic tiles.

DYE DISCS: Wax dye discs are available in a range of basic colors and can be mixed to form myriad other shades. The amount needed to achieve the basic color is recommended on the packet by the manufacturer, but for small quantities of wax it is more a matter of trial and error. Feel free to combine colors, or use as much or as little as you like to create the exact shade you want.

Dye disc colors are not as stable as dye powders, which means adjacent colors may bleed in time.

DYE POWDERS: These are very strong and are usually used for commercial candlemaking. Only a very small amount is required to achieve an intense shade. These powders in particular are used to color jelly wax.

SCENTS: Scents that can be used for candlemaking come in various forms and need to be oil-based so that they will dissolve in wax. Alcohol-based scents should not be used. Fragrance oils and scented wax beads are specially produced for candlemaking and therefore do not affect the burning properties of the candle. To obtain correct quantities, simply follow the manufacturer's instructions. Aromatherapy essential oils and dried or fresh herbs, flowers, and spices are natural materials and may not always combine properly with the wax or burn well, so small quantities need to be tested first. The project on pages 72–74, Essential Scents, uses some tried and tested oils that work well with wax.

Once you have chosen your scent, simply add it to the molten wax before pouring it into a mold. The aroma is released when the candle burns.

making candles

The essential principles of candlemaking are much the same as they were in ages past. Of course modern technology has provided us with far superior materials and equipment, but the basic rules remain the same. Candles can be made with or without molds and in myriad colors, shapes, and textures. The following simple techniques form the basis upon which nearly all the projects in this book are designed. As candlemaking is a very creative craft (and sometimes for the beginner an unpredictable one), the projects serve not only to instruct but also to inspire new candlemakers to add their own individuality, create their own colors, or design their own unique molds, using many of the following techniques as a guide.

calculating quantities of paraffin wax and stearin

Remember that it is always better to heat too much wax rather than too little, since you can keep any leftover wax and remelt it for other projects. As you become used to working with wax, you will be able to judge approximate quantities by eye, but there is a basic general formula to follow when calculating the amount of wax you will need. Fill the mold you intend to use with water, then pour the water into a measuring jug. As a guide, 5 fl oz (100 ml) of liquid is approximately equivalent to 5 oz (100 g) in weight. For every 5 fl oz (100 ml) of water you will need to use 4½ oz (90 g) of paraffin wax and ½ oz (10 g) of stearin. You need to mix 90 percent paraffin wax and 10 percent stearin. If you are working with flexible molds, you do not need to add stearin, so you should measure out 100 percent paraffin wax. If you are using commercially prepared wax, you should also measure out 100 percent prepared wax.

When you are making multicolored candles, the total amount must be divided into the various colors. When using jelly wax, you need to judge by eye how much wax you will need to fill the mold, and then cut off the required amount accordingly.

heating the stearin

Place the required amount of stearin in a double boiler and melt it until it has turned into a clear liquid. You do not use stearin in flexible molds.

adding dyes to the stearin or wax

A guide to using dye discs is given by the manufacturer, but generally a whole disc will color about 4½ lb (2 kg) of wax. To color smaller quantities, some trial and error is required. Dye discs can be cut into small pieces with a sharp knife and then crushed with the back of a spoon. Always add a small amount at a time, then increase the amount if you want a darker shade. Test the color with a strip of wax paper. Simply dip the strip into the stearin; when it dries, you will be able to see the approximate finished shade.

If you are working with a flexible mold and therefore not using stearin, simply add the dye to the wax alone and test the color in the same way.

adding the wax

Add the required amount of wax to the stearin and dye mixture, and heat them in the double boiler until molten.

adding perfume

If you are making a scented candle, this is the stage at which you add your scents. Simply add a few drops to the molten wax.

coloring jelly wax

Powder dyes are extremely strong and are usually reserved for commercial usage, when large quantities of wax need to be dyed. However, if you are using jelly wax, this is the best type of dye to use. Only a very tiny amount is necessary to achieve a very strong color. The color you see in the boiler is pretty much the finished color that will be achieved (1). Take care not to spill any onto clothes or work surfaces, as it will stain badly and will be difficult to remove.

testing the temperature

Heat paraffin wax to the temperature specified in your project. Leave the thermometer in the wax and do not overheat the wax, as it could catch on fire. As a general rule, wax used with rigid plastic, glass, and cardboard molds should be heated to 180°F (82°C). Wax used with flexible latex molds should be heated to 200°F (93°C).

Heat jelly wax just until it is molten.

priming the wick

Cut the required length of wick for your project, then dip it into the molten wax in the double boiler (2). Lay it out flat on a piece of wax paper. The wax will quickly set, and

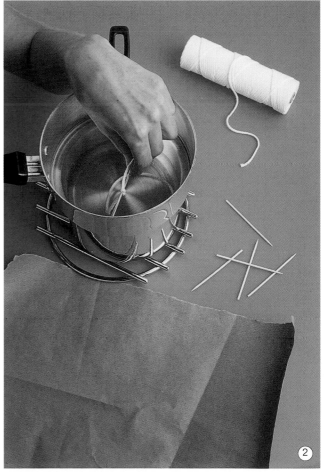

the wick will become hard and stiff. It is now ready to use. Priming stiffens the wick, ensures that it will burn properly and allows it to protrude at the top of the candle. Priming can be done in advance; you may want to prime a whole length of wick to have it ready to use.

You should not prime the wick when working with a flexible latex mold, since using an unprimed wick decreases the risk of wax spills.

positioning the wick

When using a rigid mold, cut the wick about 2 in (5 cm) longer than the height of the finished candle, prime it, and pass it through the hole at the base of the mold. Secure the wick to a suitable wick support resting across the shoulder of the mold. Pull the wick taut at the base, then secure and seal it with a small blob of mold sealer.

When using a flexible mold, again, cut the wick about 2 in (5 cm) longer than the height of the finished candle, and thread a wicking needle with the unprimed wick. Gently push the needle through the base of the mold. Seal the wick with mold sealer and secure it to a suitable wick support resting across the shoulder of the mold.

multiwick candles

Candles that have a large diameter or width, or an unusual shape, often require more than one wick so that the wax will burn evenly. Suspend two or more lengths of primed wick across the top of your mold using suitable wick supports, making sure the wicks are evenly spaced apart (3).

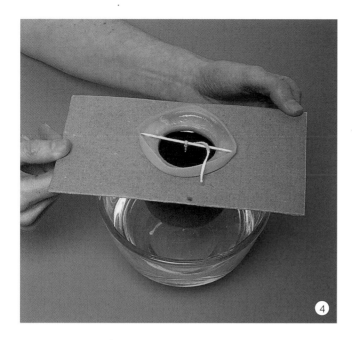

supporting a flexible mold

To secure a flexible mold over a water bath while filling it with wax, you will need some stiff cardboard that is wider than the mouth of the water bath. Cut a hole in the center of the cardboard just large enough for the top of the mold to fit in, and drop the mold into the support.

filling the mold

Whether you are using a flexible or rigid mold, fill it just over the shoulder with molten wax. Keep excess wax for topping it off later. After a minute or two, gently tap the sides of the mold to release any trapped air bubbles. Now carefully lower the mold into the water bath, avoiding splashes. A flexible mold is supported by cardboard around the shoulder of the mold and across the top of the bath (4). A rigid mold can have a weight placed on it. Allow the wax to cool.

topping it off

After about one hour, pierce the wax around the wick with a cocktail stick. Then top it off with wax reheated to the previous temperature and allow it to cool completely.

removing the candle from the mold

If you are using a rigid mold, remove the mold sealer when the candle is cold, and let the candle slide out. Trim the wick with a craft knife, and then stand the candle in a warm, empty double boiler to level off the base. Trim the revealed wick to ½ in (1 cm). It is now ready to light.

If you are using a flexible mold, wait until the wax is completely set, then remove the mold from the water bath and rub a little liquid soap all over the surface. Remove the mold sealer and gently peel the mold away from the wax, releasing the candle (5). Trim away any excess wax from around the shoulder using a craft knife.

storing unused wax

Excess wax should be poured into a bowl lined with wax paper. When it is completely cold, it can be stored in a plastic bag and then reheated and used at a later stage.

making your own molds

There are several methods you can use to make your own unique candle molds. Using a found container, such as a yogurt container or a salad bowl, is a popular choice. Geometrical molds can be formed from cardboard, while more intricate shapes can be made using a latex mold-making kit.

using found containers

Practically any watertight container, such as tin cans, cardboard tubes, yogurt containers, milk or juice cartons, glass jars, salad bowls, and even coconut shells, can be used as a mold. The only consideration to be made is the

shape. The mold should either have straight sides or sides tapering toward the base. Using a mold that tapers toward the top is not entirely impractical, but it does mean that the mold must be broken to release the candle.

Pierce a hole at the base of the mold and pass the primed wick through, then seal the hole with mold sealer. Alternatively, for more solid molds, drop in a primed wick attached to a wick sustainer. Cast the candle using wax heated to 180°F (82°C). It may be necessary to cut a cardboard or plastic mold to release the candle when set.

making a flexible mold

A flexible rubber mold can easily be made using a nonporous object as a master. Place the object on a small, upturned saucer or dish, then, following the manufacturer's instructions, apply several coats of latex mold-making solution using a paintbrush. Allow each coat to dry between applications. You will need to build up a coat about ⅛ in (3 mm) thick. For the last coat, mix the latex with the thickener provided in a ratio of 20:1. When the latex is dry, carefully peel it away from the master. Pierce a hole at the base of the mold and pass the unprimed wick through, then seal the hole with mold sealer. Cast the candle using wax without stearin heated to 200°F (93°C).

using open-ended containers

Open-ended cardboard or plastic tubes, such as packaging materials or piping, can be used to make pillar candles. Place the tube on a small piece of cardboard and seal it around the base with mold sealer. Pierce a hole in the base using a wicking needle and thread the primed wick through (1). Cast the candle as usual, using wax heated to 180°F (82°C). When the wax is cool, slice the tube open using a craft knife to release the candle.

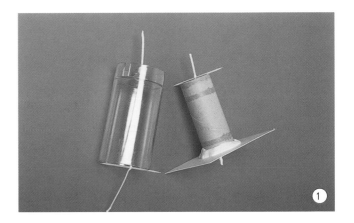

making your own cardboard mold

Rigid molds can be made using stiff or corrugated cardboard. Simply bend it to the required shape using the templates provided, or design your own shape. Score and fold the cardboard to construct the shape and fix overlaps in place using double-sided adhesive tape (2). Seal the joins with packing tape and wrap the entire mold with packing tape for added protection against leakage (3). Pierce a hole or holes in the base and thread the primed wick through, then seal with mold sealer (4). Cast the candle as usual, using wax heated to 180°F (82°C), and allow it to cool. Then use a craft knife to slice open the mold to release the candle.

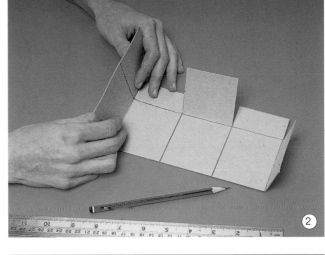

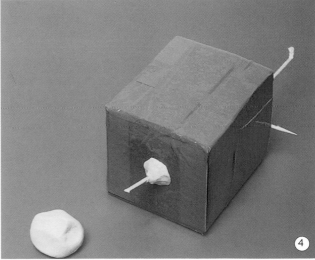

special effects

crackled candles

This delicate, crackled effect can be applied over any set, smooth-sided candle. The finish is particularly effective when used over a deeply colored candle.

Add enough uncolored paraffin wax to fill a dipping can to about 90 percent capacity – enough to cover the height of the finished candle without spilling over the edges of the can when you dip it in. Heat to 190°F (88°C). Fill a bucket with cold water and add ice cubes to turn the water icy cold. Transfer the uncolored paraffin wax to the dipping can. Hold the candle firmly by the wick and dip it once into the molten wax. Immediately plunge the candle into the bucket of ice cold water. Upon removal you will see tiny crackles appearing all over the surface.

frosted candles

This popular effect is created very simply by pouring the wax at a very low temperature into the mold.

When the wax has melted, remove it from the heat and allow it to cool, stirring continuously to prevent a skin from forming on the surface. As the wax cools and you stir briskly, you will see a little scum forming on the surface. Now pour a little wax into the prepared mold and swirl it around to coat the sides. Pour the wax back into the pan and stir it again until it's frothy. Fill the mold with frothy wax and top it off with wax cooled to 150°F (65°C).

embedded candles

Three-dimensional objects, such as shells and dried flowers, leaves, and sliced fruit, can be embedded into soft wax in the mold so that they can be viewed from the outside when the candle is released.

Cast the candle in the usual way. After about 10 minutes a thick skin, about ½ in (1 cm) thick, will have formed on top of the wax. Cut a hole in the skin with a sharp knife, and pour the still-molten wax in the center back into the double boiler. Working quickly while the

wax at the edges of the mold is still soft, press the pieces to be embedded firmly and deeply into the soft wax (1). Allow the wax to set. Remelt the wax in the double boiler and pour it back into the mold at a temperature no higher than 165°F (73°C). Leave it to set.

encrusted candles

You can cover the outside of your candle with decorative objects that are partly embedded in the wax.

First, make an ordinary candle. Place this candle inside a second mold that is slightly wider than the first candle and resupport the wick as usual. Pour or spoon your chosen objects (such as grains or glass nuggets) between the sides of the two molds. Remelt more paraffin wax to 180°F (82°C) and spoon it into the gap, to a height just above the first candle. Leave the candle to set as usual.

embossed candles

An embossed effect can be achieved by gluing three-dimensional, decorative plastic moldings or thick cardboard cutouts to the inside walls of a cardboard mold before casting.

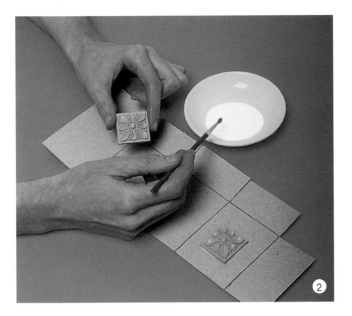

First, cut out and score lines on the mold to be used. Use a household waterproof glue to fix the molding or cutouts to one or all of the side walls, on the inside of the mold (2). Alternatively, cardboard that is already embossed with a three-dimensional pattern can be used to make or line the mold. Make up the mold and cast the candle as usual. When the wax is cold, slice open the mold using a craft knife to release the candle.

ice candles

This unusual effect is created by surrounding a ready-made candle in a slightly wider mold with crushed ice and molten wax.

Use a ready-made candle that is a little shorter and narrower than your mold and no less than 1 in (2.5 cm) in diameter. Cut the candle to fit the mold, if necessary. Place the candle in the mold and tie the wick to a suitable wick support. Do not seal the hole at the base of the mold. Fill the mold surrounding the candle with coarsely crushed ice, and stand the mold in an empty bowl or on a plate that will catch the water as it melts. Pour in the prepared wax, heated to 210°F (99°C), and allow the candle to cool (3).

pineapple candles

This interesting textured effect is very simply achieved by cooling a little wax in a bowl of cold water so that the wax turns into brittle strands.

Prepare the mold and heat the wax as usual. Pour some of the wax in a steady stream into a bowl of cold water. The wax will solidify and form irregular strands on contact with the water. Take out the wax strands and pack them loosely in the mold. Let the remaining wax cool to about 150°F (65°C), then fill the mold as usual. Top it off with wax cooled to the same temperature.

striped candles

Different colored waxes may be used to make a striped or layered candle. It is best to use a clear plastic mold for this, so that you can see the levels. If you want to use a specially designed cardboard mold, simply make small marks on the outside with a pen or masking tape to guide you as you fill the mold.

Mix up your colored wax and heat it to 180°F (82°C). Fill the mold to the height required. After a few minutes, gently tap the mold to release any air bubbles. Allow the first layer of wax to set until the surface feels rubbery to the touch. While you are waiting, heat another colored wax to the same temperature. Pour the second layer onto the rubbery first stripe. Continue in the same way until you have built up the desired amount of layers. Top off the final layer and leave the candle to cool as usual.

safety

Candlemaking is a relatively simple craft that can be done safely in your own kitchen, but it is important to follow a few necessary safety guidelines to avoid accidents and possible injury.

heating wax

Candle wax should be treated in the same way and with the same precautions as cooking oil, in that it should never be overheated or left unattended while it's being heated. Always heat wax in a double boiler, as this ensures that the temperature does not exceed 212°F (100°C). Also, monitor the temperature regularly and carefully with a thermometer.

If the wax is heated to a temperature greater than 212°F (100°C), it begins to smoke and is then in real danger of ignition. In such an event, turn off the heat source immediately, and then smother the flames with a damp towel or saucepan lid. Do not try to extinguish the flames with water.

preparing the work area

Cover your work surfaces with sheets of newspaper, to keep your kitchen counter clean and to catch drips and spills. When pouring hot wax into prepared molds, it can be helpful to place the mold on a cookie sheet or flat dish, just in case the mold leaks. Also this means that you can save the leaked wax for later use.

Keep molds and equipment clean. Wash them in hot, soapy water immediately after use, but remember to never pour wax down the sink, as it will solidify and block the pipe.

Finally, try to keep all your equipment and materials within reach; it is essential that you do not leave the wax unattended while you look for that essential item.

treating spills

It is advisable, but not necessary, to wear an apron while making candles, just in case something spills. Usually wax can be removed from clothing by ironing the garment between two sheets of brown paper that will absorb the wax. If wax falls onto the floor or a hard surface, just leave it to solidify, then scrape it off using a spatula, or lift off small spots with your fingernail. A point to remember, however, is that some waxes are strongly colored and may leave a stain behind.

using candles safely

After all your hard work, it is now time to enjoy the fruits of your labor. There are just a few points to mention. Never leave a burning candle unattended, and remember to place candles in a safe position away from drafts or soft furnishings, curtains, or any other flammable material. Always allow ample headroom above the candle flame for the heat to disperse – a point to remember if you have candles on shelves.

Be sure to choose the right candle holder. Use one that is steady and not likely to tip over, and make sure that it is heat resistant. If using a holder with a spike, heat the spike with a match first; this will prevent the base of the candle from splitting when it is pushed into place.

Never burn a candle near another heat source or electrical equipment.

Remember to keep candles well out of the reach of children and pets.

To extinguish a candle, it is best to use a candle snuffer rather than to just blow out the flame. If the candle is large or in a container, there may be a well of molten wax formed around the wick. In this case, after the flame is extinguished, use a cocktail stick or a matchstick to push the wick briefly into the wax so it is reprimed and ready to use the next time.

Trim the candle wick before lighting and relighting it; if the wick is longer than about ½ in (1 cm), the flame may smoke.

Always leave your newly made candles to rest for at least one day before lighting them.

subtle slim

In the first section we learned about the joys of candlemaking in the simplest of forms. The following projects have been grouped together because they all possess an element of simplicity and pureness. As an introduction to candlemaking, they require very little in the way of complicated technical knowledge.

We begin with slim jims. These smooth, simple, and elegant forms are cast from undyed wax in cardboard molds. Then we move on to fragrant hand-rolled beeswax pillars, which require no mold or heating at all. Slender bamboo candles will show you how easy it is to make a flexible mold to produce an unusual, individualized shape. The green apple candles also use a flexible mold, but this time it is a ready-made one. These candles use commercially prepared dye complete with apple scent. Jelly wax is a relatively new product that enables the candlemaker to produce a stunning, transparent candle contained in a simple glass vase. Egg candles will show you what can be created using ready-made molds. After these projects are under your belt, you will have mastered the basic techniques of candlemaking.

plicity

slim jims

The slender elegance of these oval candles is further enhanced by their simplicity and the minimalistic use of undyed wax. Make them in a range of different sizes and use them in a grouped display that will look beautiful even when unlit.

materials

tracing paper
stiff, shiny cardboard
1½ in (4 cm) diameter wick and a wick sustainer
1½ oz (35 g) stearin
13½ oz (315 g) paraffin wax

additional equipment

pencil and scissors
ruler
double-sided adhesive tape
packing tape

PREPARING THE MOLD: Using tracing paper, photocopy the templates given on page 76 at 200 percent. Transfer the designs to cardboard and cut them out. Score and fold them along the dotted lines using a ruler. Make sure the shiny surface of the cardboard is facing inward. Fold the rectangle around the oval base and fix it in position using double-sided adhesive tape at the base of the rectangle. Seal the joins with packing tape. Put your hand inside the mold and open it up a little to form the slim oval shape. To make sure it is leakproof, wrap the entire mold with packing tape. Place the mold on a cookie sheet and fix it in place around the base using mold sealer. This will also prevent any wax from leaking out.

PREPARING THE WICK: Cut the wick about 2 in (5 cm) longer than the height of the finished candle and prime it (see page 17). Attach one end to a wick sustainer. Drop the wick into the mold and thread the free end through a cocktail stick or tie it to a wooden skewer. Rest the stick across the top of the mold so that it holds the wick vertically down the center.

PREPARING THE WAX: Melt the stearin in a double boiler. Add the paraffin wax and continue to heat until the wax is molten and reaches a temperature of 180°F (82°C).

FORMING THE CANDLE: Pour the wax into the center of the mold and set it aside. Keep the excess wax for topping off later. After a few minutes, gently tap the sides of the mold to release any trapped air bubbles. Transfer the candle to a water bath and weigh it down. After about an hour, a dip will form around the wick. Pierce the wax a few times with a cocktail stick, then top off with wax reheated to 180°F (82°C). Leave it to set completely.

FINISHING: Remove the mold sealer and slice the mold open with a craft knife to release the candle. Remove the wick support and trim the revealed wick to about ½ in (1 cm).

To make the larger candle, photocopy the templates at 350 percent and use 2½ oz (65 g) of stearin and 22½ oz (585 g) of paraffin wax.

tip

Candles made in cardboard molds can have a cloudy or matte appearance. To achieve a soft sheen, simply buff the surface of the candle firmly with a soft cloth.

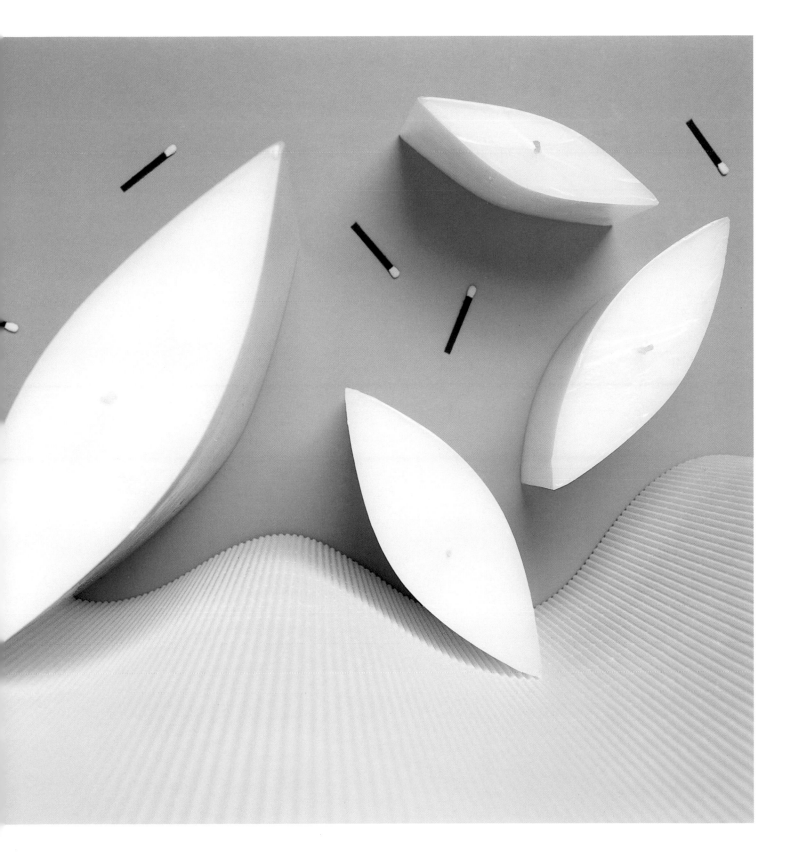

naturally beeswax

Rolling sheets of preformed, natural beeswax is probably the simplest and cleanest way of making candles. It takes almost no time and requires very little equipment to create these beautiful and stylish candles. The triangular shape chosen for this project is an alternative to the usual round form, but it is just as easy to make. Beeswax has a wonderful honeylike fragrance and, at room temperature, is soft, pliable, and extremely easy to work with. No heating or gluing is required. The honeycomb texture and slightly tacky surface of each sheet enable the wax to stick to itself; only slight pressure from your hand is necessary to shape and hold the candle together.

materials
2 in (5 cm) diameter wick
4 beeswax sheets

additional equipment
metal ruler

PREPARING THE WICK: Cut a length of wick about ¾ in (2 cm) longer than the height of the finished candle and prime it (see page 17). Press the wick firmly onto the short-sided edge of one beeswax sheet.

ROLLING: Carefully curl the edge of the beeswax sheet tightly around the wick, and then begin rolling up the whole sheet. When you reach the end, gently press the edge of the sheet into the rolled surface underneath.

SHAPING: Lay the candle along the length of a metal ruler. Press the ruler against the candle to make a flat side, then turn the candle and repeat, making another flat side at roughly a 60-degree angle to the first. Repeat once more, again at an approximately 60-degree angle, to create a softly rounded triangular shape. Press firmly along the length of all three sides with your fingers to make sure that there are no gaps and that the sides are fairly smooth.

BUILDING UP: Lay another sheet of beeswax right up to the edge of the first sheet and press the two edges firmly together. Continue to roll up the sheet as before, following the triangular shape. Make sure that you roll evenly, so that all the edges remain at the same height. Reshape the candles using the ruler as necessary.

FINISHING: Add on the remaining two sheets in the same way until the candle is complete. If you want to make a candle that is larger in diameter, simply add on more sheets.
   To make a more squat shape, use three sheets cut in half lengthways, thus creating six pieces in all.

tip

When making this type of candle, keep the beeswax warm, or it will tend to crack. Average room temperature is sufficient to keep the wax pliable, but if you do experience any problems, simply warm the sheets up a little using a hair dryer.

best bamboo

Making your own flexible mold is the only way to produce candles that are an unusual shape or have a delicate surface pattern. Latex mold-making materials are readily available and quite easy to use. For this project, use chunky lengths of bamboo as a master mold and you can make as many beautifully shaped candles as you like.

materials
8 in (20 cm) length of bamboo 1½ in (4 cm) in diameter
1½ in (4 cm) diameter wick
stiff cardboard
9½ oz (270 g) paraffin wax
¹⁄₁₀ of a green dye disc
liquid soap

additional equipment
sandpaper
small saucer
mold-making kit containing a latex mold-making solution
    and thickener
paintbrush
scissors

MAKING THE MOLD: Sand the cut edges of the bamboo length to ensure that there are no rough edges. Fill the hollow ends using mold sealer to prevent the mold-making solution from going down inside the bamboo. Stand the piece of bamboo on a small, upturned saucer and fix it in place with some more mold sealer. Following the manufacturer's instructions, apply several coats of the latex mold-making solution to the bamboo and saucer. You can either paint the solution on with a brush or spoon it over the master. Allow each coat to dry before applying the next one. You will need to build up a layer about ⅛ in (3 mm) thick. For the last coat, mix the latex with the thickener in a ratio of 20:1, then stir it well. When the mixture has thickened, apply the final coat and set it

aside. When it is completely dry, carefully peel the mold away from the master. Prepare a water bath that can contain the length of the candle.

PREPARING THE WICK AND MOLD: Cut an unprimed wick about 2 in (5 cm) longer than the height of the finished candle and thread it through the eye of a wicking needle. Carefully pierce a hole at the base of the latex mold and draw the wick through. Seal the wick in place with mold sealer.

Fashion a support for the rubbery mold using stiff cardboard that is wider than the neck of the water bath. Carefully cut a hole in the center of the cardboard, just large enough to fit around the shoulder of the mold. Place the mold in the cardboard support, then pass a cocktail stick through the wick. Let the stick lie across the shoulder of the mold, holding it vertically in the center of the mold.

PREPARING THE WAX: Place the wax in a double boiler and heat it to 200°F (93°C). Prepare the small amount of green dye disc to achieve the pale coloring, then crush it roughly with the back of a spoon. Add the crushed dye to the molten wax and stir until it is dissolved. The greater the amount of dye used, the stronger the color will be, so start with a small amount and add more later, if necessary. To get an idea of the approximate finished shade, dip a piece of wax paper into the dyed wax and allow it to dry.

FORMING THE CANDLE: Rest the cardboard support over an empty container and carefully pour the wax into the mold, filling it to the shoulder. Keep the excess wax for topping it off later. After a few minutes, gently tap the sides of the mold to release any trapped air bubbles. Lower the filled mold into the water bath with the cardboard supporting it, and set it aside for about an hour. As the wax sets, a dip will form around the wick. Pierce the wax a few times around the wick with a cocktail stick to prevent distortion. After another hour, top it off with wax reheated to 200°F (93°C). Return the mold to the water bath until the wax is completely set.

FINISHING: Remove the mold from the cardboard support and cover the outside with liquid soap to facilitate easy removal. Carefully pull the rubber mold back on itself, releasing the bamboo-shaped candle. Ease the wick from the base gently, so you don't damage the mold. Use a craft knife to trim any excess wax and wick from the base of the candle, leveling off any unevenness. Trim the revealed wick to about ½ in (1 cm).

green apples

Using flexible commercial molds is an easy way to produce irregularly shaped candles or, in this case, very realistic fruit-shaped candles. However, there are a few things to remember when using flexible molds. The wick must be unprimed, since this decreases the risk of wax seepage. The mold will need to be supported by a rigid cardboard template while the wax sets, ideally in a water bath, and stearin should not be used in the wax for this project, as it will eventually rot the rubber mold.

materials
1 ¼ in (3 cm) diameter wick
stiff cardboard
8 ½ oz (240 g) paraffin wax
approximately ⅟₇ of an apple-scented green dye disc
liquid soap

additional equipment
scissors
apple-shaped flexible latex mold
soft cloth

PREPARING THE WICK AND MOLD: Cut the unprimed wick about 2 in (5 cm) longer than the mold and thread it through the eye of a wicking needle. Draw the needle and wick through the base of the mold, leaving a tail of ⅝ in (1.5 cm). This will eventually be the "stalk" of the finished apple candle. Seal it in place with mold sealer. Fashion a support for the flexible mold using stiff cardboard that is wider than the mouth of the water bath. Carefully cut a hole in the center of the cardboard, just large enough to fit around the collar of the mold. Place the mold into the cardboard support, then thread a cocktail stick through the wick and rest the stick across the shoulder of the mold, holding the wick vertically in the center.

PREPARING THE WAX: Place the wax in a double boiler and heat it to 200°F (93°C). Crush the apple-scented green dye with the back of a spoon. This is enough for one candle. Add the crushed dye to the molten wax and stir it in.

FORMING THE CANDLE: Rest the cardboard support over an empty container and pour the dyed wax into the mold, filling it to the shoulder. Keep the excess wax for topping it off later. After a few minutes, gently tap the sides of the mold to release any trapped air bubbles. Transfer the mold to a water bath, with the cardboard supporting it. After about an hour, a dip will form around the wick. Use a cocktail stick to pierce the wax a few times around the wick. After another hour has elapsed, reheat the excess wax to 200°F (93°C) and use it to top off the mold. Set the candle aside until the wax is completely cool.

FINISHING: Lift the mold from the support and remove the mold sealer and wick support. Cover the outside of the mold with liquid soap, then carefully pull the mold back on itself, easing the wick gently from the base so as not to damage the mold. Use a craft knife to trim any excess wax and wick from the base, leveling off any unevenness so the fruit will stand steadily by itself. Trim the revealed wick to about ½ in (1 cm). Finally, buff the wax to a subtle sheen using a soft cloth.

tip

Changing the water in the water bath about every 15 minutes during the first two hours will speed up the setting process.

jelly jar

Jelly wax is a relatively new product that can be used to create some really stunning visual effects. When the wax sets it looks and feels like jelly, and thus cannot be cast in a conventional mold, but instead should be supported in a decorative glass container.

materials
4 in (10 cm) diameter wick and a wick sustainer
35 oz (1 kg) jelly wax
pinch of violet powdered dye
glitter (optional)

additional equipment
saucepan
glass container, 4 in (10 cm) in diameter and
        7 in (18 cm) in height

PREPARING THE WICK: Begin by cutting the wick about 2 in (5 cm) taller than the glass. Prime the wick as usual (see page 17). Thread one end of the wick into a wick sustainer. Place a tiny blob of mold sealer on the underside of the wick sustainer, then press it firmly to the base of the vase. Lay a wooden skewer across the top of the vase and tie the wick securely to it.

PREPARING THE WAX: Melt about 8¾ oz (250 g) of jelly wax in a double boiler over low heat. The wax will begin to melt slowly. It is important not to try to speed up the process by increasing the heat, as the wax will quickly become too hot and begin to smoke. Stir occasionally, and when all the wax is molten and fluid, add the violet powder a tiny speck at a time. This dye is intended for commercial use and is very concentrated. Fortunately, the color does not change when the jelly sets, so it is easy to judge the amount of dye to put in. When you are happy with the shade, remove the pan from the heat.

FORMING THE CANDLE: Place a folded kitchen towel around the outside of the glass container to catch any drips. Pour the colored jelly wax carefully into the vase and allow it to set for about 15 minutes. While the wax is still molten in the vase you can sprinkle in some glitter for added effect. Repeat the process with another 8¾ oz (250 g) of wax, but this time put in only about half the quantity of dye previously used. Pour the wax into the vase and allow it to set as before. Then melt the remaining wax with no dye and pour it into the vase, only up to about 1¼ in (3 cm) from the top. Put the candle aside to set completely. Watch the shades merge, creating quite amazing color changes.

FINISHING: When the candle is cool, snip off the wick about ¾ in (2 cm) above the top of the wax. Remember that neither the wick nor the flame should protrude above the top of the container.

tip

To achieve good, transparent colors, it is important to use powdered dye for this project rather than conventional dye discs, since technically the jelly is not "wax."

free-range eggs

Spherical or egg-shaped candles are easily formed by using ready-made, two-part molds that are available in a variety of sizes. Here, the distinctive shape has been cast using three minimally different amounts of dye to create pale, midtone, and dark candles that look realistically egglike. The following technique describes the amounts of wax and stearin needed to make a single egg candle, but you may find it easier to make more eggs using larger amounts of wax and stearin.

materials

1 in (2.5 cm) diameter wick
⅖ oz (12 g) stearin (a ratio of 20 percent stearin to 80 percent paraffin wax is used to increase the opacity of the finished candle)
brown dye disc
1⅗ oz (48 g) paraffin wax

additional equipment

clear plastic two-part egg mold, with a stand

PREPARING THE WICK: Cut the wick about 2 in (5 cm) longer than the height of the finished candle and prime it (see page 17). Use a wicking needle to thread one end through the hole at the base of the bottom half of the mold (which will form the top part of the finished egg shape), then continue to thread it through the other half of the mold. Place the two halves of the mold together and seal around the join with mold sealer. At the base of the mold, pull the wick taut, leaving about ⅝ in (1.5 cm) revealed, and seal it with mold sealer. Pass a cocktail stick through the other end of the wick and lay the stick across the top of the mold, holding the wick vertically down the center of the mold.

PREPARING THE WAX: Melt the stearin in a double boiler. Crush a sliver of brown dye with the back of a spoon and add it to the stearin, stirring until it dissolves. To get an idea of the approximate finished shade, dip a strip of wax paper into the dyed stearin and allow it to dry. Add more dye to achieve a darker, stronger color.

Add the paraffin wax and heat until the wax is molten and reaches a temperature of 180°F (82°C).

FORMING THE CANDLE: Pour the wax into the center of the mold and keep the excess wax for topping it off later. After a few minutes, gently tap the sides of the mold to release any trapped air bubbles. Transfer the mold to a water bath and weigh it down. Leave it to set. After about an hour, a dip will form around the wick. Pierce the wax a few times with a cocktail stick, then top it off with wax reheated to 180°F (82°C). Leave it to set completely.

FINISHING: When you remove the mold sealer, the candle will slide easily out of the mold. Trim the wick at the base so the candle stands steadily, then trim the revealed end of the wick to about ½ in (1 cm).

To make darker eggs, simply add more brown dye, but add only a sliver at a time.

characte
cre

The following creations show how easy it is to achieve spectacular effects based on texture, surface decoration, and color combinations by using just a few simple techniques. Most of the projects use ready-made molds or very simple molds made from cardboard or latex.

Strange as it may seem, the ubiquitous "frosted" look is, in fact, the traditional candlemaker's nightmare. In purist terms, the effect is actually a "fault." These days, however, it is considered very attractive and is achieved simply by pouring the wax at a very low temperature, giving basic candle shapes a contemporary edge.

Temperature is the key factor in most of the special effects featured in this section. Rapid cooling of freshly cast pyramid candles in a bath of icy cold water produces a delicately crackled effect on the surface. The juicy pineapple pillars also use an icy cold bath to make molten

ristic ations

wax turn into brittle strands, producing the "pineapple" effect. Ice blue candles are cast in a plastic mold filled with crushed ice, which then melts, causing the wax to set in the form of a labyrinth of delicate cavities.

Tapered stripes and Rothko-esque candles feature the versatility of random striping of different colored waxes. The tapered shape is cast in a large glass salad bowl mold, resulting in a smooth surface, while the candle inspired by Mark Rothko is made in a cardboard mold that generally produces a soft, matte appearance.

Using the characteristic slant on surface decoration, the citrus-colored rectangular and square-shaped candles have pretty floral designs embossed on the surface, while the stone-shaped candles are enhanced with simple hand-painting techniques.

frosted cubes

A group of four frosted candle cubes nestling neatly together would make a delightful centerpiece for a table or display area. The frosted effect is easily achieved and very beautiful.

materials
2⅜ in (6 cm) diameter wick
9½ oz (270 g) commercially prepared green paraffin wax

additional equipment
masking tape
clear plastic, square-based pillar mold, 2⅜ in (6 cm)
    in width and 6½ in (16 cm) in height

PREPARING THE MOLD: This technique involves moving the mold with the wax in it, so instead of filling a square mold to the top and therefore spilling the wax, you need to use a mold that is taller than the height of the finished candle. Simply mark the correct level by placing a strip of masking tape on the outside of the mold at a height of 2⅜ in (6 cm) from the base.

PREPARING THE WICK: Cut the wick about 2 in (5 cm) longer than the height of the finished candle and prime it (see page 17). Use a wicking needle to thread the wick through the hole at the base of the mold. Tie the end of the wick to a wooden skewer. Rest the stick across the top of the mold, holding the wick vertically down the center. At the base of the mold pull the wick taut, and then seal it with mold sealer.

tips

Remember that the frosting effect causes the wax to appear much lighter in color, so take this into consideration when choosing your colored wax.
  If finished candles differ in height, just stand each in a warm, empty double boiler to melt and level off the base so they will match each other exactly.

PREPARING THE WAX: Heat the commercially prepared paraffin wax in a double boiler until molten.

THE FROSTING TECHNIQUE: Remove the wax from the heat and allow it to cool, stirring continuously to prevent a skin from forming. Soon you will see a little scum developing on the surface. When this happens, pour a little wax into the mold. Swirl the wax around the mold to coat the inside, just up to the marked level, then pour the wax back into the pan. Briskly stir the wax again until it becomes frothy. Refill the mold up to the mark and keep the excess wax for topping it off later. After a few minutes, tap the sides of the mold to release any trapped air bubbles that could ruin the finished effect. Transfer the mold to a water bath and weigh it down. After about an hour, a dip will form around the wick. Pierce the wax a few times around the wick with a cocktail stick, then top it off to the marked level with molten wax cooled to a temperature of no greater than 150°F (65°C). Leave it to set completely.

FINISHING: The cold candle will slide easily out of the mold when the mold sealer is removed. Trim the wick at the base so that the candle stands steadily, then remove the wick support and snip the revealed wick to about ½ in (1 cm).
  To complete the set, make another green frosted candle and two blue ones in exactly the same way.

tapered stripes

These chunky tapered shapes were inspired by simple glass salad bowls, which can be found in many sizes and were actually used here as molds. The striped candle was built by layering red and undyed wax, which takes on the color of the surrounding red layers to create an individual pink shade. Any container can be used in the same way, provided it is fairly rigid and watertight. A candle of this size needs more than one wick to ensure that the wax burns evenly.

materials

½ in (13 mm) diameter wick and 3 wick sustainers
7 oz (200 g) stearin
2 red dye discs
4 lb (1.8 kg) paraffin wax (for the red layers)
2 oz (60 g) stearin
19 oz (540 g) paraffin wax (for the middle layer)

additional equipment

tapered glass salad bowl, approximately 3¼ in (8 cm) in
  diameter at the base, 8 in (20 cm) in diameter at the
  top, and 4¾ in (12 cm) in height
masking tape

PREPARING THE WICK: Cut three wicks about 2 in (5 cm) longer than the height of the finished candle and prime them (see page 17). Attach one end of each primed wick to a wick sustainer. Drop the wicks into the mold, evenly spaced apart, and tie the free ends to two or three wooden skewers. Lay the sticks across the top of the salad bowl mold, so that they hold the wicks vertically inside the mold.

PREPARING THE WAX: Melt the first quantity of stearin in a double boiler. Crush both red dye discs with the back of a spoon. Add the crushed dye to the melted stearin and stir it to dissolve. To test the color, dip a strip of wax paper into the dyed stearin. When it dries, you will be able to see an approximate finished shade. Add more dye to make a deeper, darker color.

Add the first quantity of paraffin wax to the dyed stearin and continue to heat until the wax is molten and reaches a temperature of 180°F (82°C).

FORMING THE CANDLE: Mark the outside of the salad bowl with masking tape strips indicating the height of each stripe you want to make. The first mark here is approximately 2 in (5 cm) up from the base of the bowl and the second mark is approximately 1¼ in (3 cm) above that. Pour the red wax into the center of the mold and fill it to the first mark. Retain the excess for the final layer. Set the mold aside for a few minutes, then gently tap the sides to release any trapped air bubbles. Allow the wax to set until it is quite rubbery to the touch.

While the first layer is setting, mix up a batch of undyed wax, using the second quantity of stearin and paraffin wax. As soon as the first layer has set to a

rubbery consistency, pour in the middle layer of undyed wax, filling the mold up to the second mark. Allow it to set as the first layer did. To get the red wax to blend in with the undyed wax, it is essential that you do not let each layer of wax set too solidly. Finally, add another layer of red wax to almost fill the mold. Keep excess wax

for topping it off later. After about an hour, a dip will form around the wicks. Pierce the wax a few times with a cocktail stick, then top it off with wax reheated to 180°F (82°C). Leave it to set completely.

FINISHING: When the wax is cold, the candle will easily slide out of the mold. Remove the wick supports and trim the wicks down to ½ in (1 cm).

To make the solid-colored tapered candles, use a salad bowl approximately 4 in (10 cm) in diameter at the base, 10 in (25 cm) in diameter at the top, and 6 in (15 cm) tall. Use 10 oz (300 g) of stearin, 6 lb 6 oz (2.7 kg) of paraffin wax, and six red dye discs for the claret candle or two red dye discs for the paler candle.

tip

You can, of course, make several candles in different sizes and with varying color combinations. Cream looks good interspersed between colors, and candles formed using different shades of just one color are also very attractive.

crackled pyramids

All that is required to produce this dramatic effect is a bucket of icy cold water. Dip a set candle once in the uncolored paraffin wax, then plunge it immediately into the water. The sudden change in temperature causes the outer layer of uncolored wax to shatter, producing a delicate pattern of tiny crackles all over the surface, which looks almost ceramic in appearance. The effect is more pronounced on a strongly colored candle, so for this project a deep rich amber is mixed using two commercial, precolored waxes.

materials
2 in (5 cm) diameter wick
7 oz (200 g) commercially prepared yellow paraffin wax
3 oz (90 g) commercially prepared red paraffin wax
ice cubes
32 oz (900 g) uncolored paraffin wax

additional equipment
clear plastic pyramid mold, 2⅜ in (6 cm) wide
    and 9 in (23 cm) high
35 oz (1 kg) capacity dipping can
large bowl
kitchen towel

PREPARING THE WICK: Cut the wick to about 2 in (5 cm) longer than the height of the finished candle and prime it (see page 17). Use a wicking needle to draw the wick through the hole at the base of the mold. Pull the wick taut at the base, leaving about ⅝ in (1.5 cm) revealed, and seal it with mold sealer. Tie the other end of the wick around a wooden skewer and rest the stick across the shoulder of the mold, holding the wick vertically down the center of the mold.

PREPARING THE WAX: Put both the yellow and the red commercially prepared waxes into a double boiler and heat them until the wax is molten and reaches a temperature of 180°F (82°C).

FORMING THE CANDLE: Pour the wax into the mold and set it aside. Keep the excess wax for topping it off later. After a few minutes, gently tap the sides of the mold to release any trapped air bubbles. Transfer the mold to a water bath and weigh it down. After about an hour, a dip will form around the wick. Pierce the wax a few times with a cocktail stick. After another hour has elapsed, reheat the wax left in the boiler to 180°F (82°C) and use it to top off the mold. Leave it to set completely. Remove the mold sealer and slide the candle out of the mold. Do not trim the wick yet.

THE CRACKLING TECHNIQUE: Add ice cubes to a bucket of cold water. Leave it to stand for a few minutes, so that the water becomes ice cold. Heat the uncolored paraffin wax in a clean double boiler to a temperature of 190°F (88°C). Carefully transfer the wax to a dipping can. Hold the set pyramid candle firmly by the wick and dip it once into the molten wax, taking care to cover the entire candle from the tip to the base. Then immediately plunge the candle into the bucket of icy water. Keep the candle submerged for a few minutes, until the dipped layer is completely cold and set. Remove the candle and watch the cracks as they form. Dry the candle with a cloth and trim the wick at the base so the candle stands steadily. Trim the revealed wick to about ½ in (1 cm).

tip

This effect can also be achieved by placing a warm, half-set candle into the freezer. The wax will cool very rapidly, resulting in a similar crackled surface appearance; however, the crackles will be much larger.

pineapple pillars

These juicy, citrus-colored pillar candles look almost like crushed pineapple. The effect is created by simply pouring some hot wax into a bowl of cold water, then filling the mold with the resulting brittle strands. The rest of the mold is then refilled with molten wax as usual.

materials
3 in (7.5 cm) diameter wick
3½ oz (100 g) stearin
¼ of a yellow dye disc
31½ oz (900 g) paraffin wax

additional equipment
mold (any large, tubular, watertight
    food container, such as that used
    for stacking potato chips and dried fruit,
    approximately 2¾ in (7 cm) in diameter
    and 8 in (20 cm) in height)
scissors
bradawl
large bowl
fork

PREPARING THE MOLD: Cut the mold to size, if necessary. Using a bradawl, pierce a hole in the center of the base of the mold. Fill a large bowl with cold water for later use.

PREPARING THE WICK: Cut the wick about 2 in (5 cm) longer than the height of the finished candle and prime it (see page 17). Use a wicking needle to thread one end of the wick through the hole at the base of the mold. Pass a cocktail stick through the wick and rest the stick across the top of the mold, holding the wick vertically down the center of the mold. At the base of the mold, pull the wick taut and seal it with mold sealer.

PREPARING THE WAX: Melt the stearin in a double boiler. Crush the yellow dye with the back of a spoon and add it to the stearin, stirring to dissolve it. To get an idea of the approximate finished shade, dip a strip of wax paper into the dyed stearin and allow it to dry. Add more dye to achieve a darker, stronger color.

Add the paraffin wax and heat until the wax is molten and reaches a temperature of 180°F (82°C).

THE TEXTURING TECHNIQUE: Pour approximately half of the wax in a steady stream into the bowl of cold water. The wax cools rapidly on contact with the water, forming irregular brittle strands. Use a fork to scoop the strands out of the water, shake off the excess drips, then loosely pack them into the mold. Reheat the remaining wax until it is molten and then let it cool to about 150°F (65°C). Pour the wax into the center of the mold, filling it to the top. The refill temperature must be lower than usual, otherwise the delicate strands will melt and the effect will be ruined. Keep the excess wax for topping off later. After a few minutes, gently tap the sides of the mold to release any trapped air bubbles. After about an hour, a dip will form around the wick. Pierce the wax a few times with a cocktail stick, then top off with wax cooled to 150°F (65°C). Leave it to set completely.

FINISHING: When cold, the candle should easily slide from the mold when the mold sealer is removed. If you experience any difficulty, simply slice the mold open with a craft knife to release the candle. Trim the wick at the base so that the candle stands steadily, then remove the wick support and trim the revealed wick to ½ in (1 cm).

To make the squat orange pineapple pillar, use the same amount of wax and stearin and ⅓ of an orange dye disc in a "found" or plastic mold 4 in (10 cm) in diameter and 4¾ in (12 cm) in height. For the midsized orange textured candle, use 19 oz (540 g) of paraffin wax, 2 oz (60 g) of stearin, and ¼ of an orange dye disc. Use a plastic or "found" mold 3 in (7.5 cm) in diameter and 6½ in (16 cm) in height.

rothko-esque

The subtle, muted colors of Mark Rothko paintings were the inspiration for this rectangular, double-wicked candle. Since a cardboard mold is used for its casting, it is difficult to see how the layers are forming. However, it is exciting to open up the mold and see the finished result.

materials

tracing paper
stiff, shiny cardboard
2 in (5 cm) diameter wick
7 oz (200 g) commercially prepared dark blue paraffin wax
7 oz (200 g) commercially prepared blue paraffin wax
7 oz (200 g) commercially prepared orange paraffin wax
7 oz (200 g) commercially prepared red paraffin wax

additional equipment

pencil and scissors
ruler
double-sided adhesive tape
packing tape

PREPARING THE MOLD: Photocopy the template on page 77 at 400 percent. Trace and transfer it to stiff cardboard and cut it out. Score along the dotted lines and bend the cardboard, using a ruler, to form a rectangular box with the shiny surface facing inward. Use a pencil to clearly mark the height of each layer you want to build on the inside of the mold before taping it together. Fix the side overlap into position using double-sided adhesive tape. Fold the flaps under at the base and fix with double-sided tape. Wrap the entire mold with packing tape to seal all the joins and prevent possible seepage.

PREPARING THE WICKS: Cut two wicks about 2 in (5 cm) longer than the height of the finished candle and prime them (see page 17). Use a wicking needle to pierce two evenly spaced holes through the base of the mold, then thread one end of each wick through each hole. Tie the wick ends to a wooden skewer and lay it across the top of the mold, holding the wicks vertically. At the base of the mold, pull the wicks taut and seal them with mold sealer.

Place the mold on a cookie sheet and seal it around the base with more mold sealer to fix it in place.

PREPARING THE WAX: Melt the dark blue wax in a double boiler until it is molten and reaches a temperature of 180°F (82°C).

FORMING THE CANDLE: Pour the dark blue wax into the center of the mold up to the first pencil mark. After a few minutes, gently tap the sides of the mold to release any trapped air bubbles.

BUILDING UP LAYERS: Prepare the blue wax in the same way as before. Allow the first layer of wax to become rubbery to the touch, then pour in the second layer. After a few minutes, gently tap the mold to release any trapped air bubbles. Continue working in the same way with the orange and red waxes. Keep some excess red wax for topping off later. Set the candle aside. After about an hour, a dip will form around each wick. Pierce the surface of the wax a few times with a cocktail stick, then top it off with wax reheated to 180°F (82°C). Leave it to set.

FINISHING: When the wax is completely cold, remove the mold sealer and wick supports and slice open the mold with a craft knife. Snip off the wicks level with the base and trim the revealed wicks to ½ in (1 cm).

troubleshooting

If the stripes are undefined in the finished candle, it means that the layers were not set enough to support one another. Make sure the surface of the previous layer is rubbery to the touch before pouring on the next layer of wax.

ice blue

As the name suggests, ice candles are made with the help of ice. The molten wax is poured over crushed ice contained in a wide pillar mold that has a ready-made candle measuring 1 in (2.5 cm) in diameter as a core. The wax cools quickly, creating a fascinating labyrinth of irregular cavities. When the ice melts, the water can be poured away. The core candle protects the wick from moisture, ensuring that the candle lights and burns as usual.

materials

blue ready-made candle, 1 in (2.5 cm) in diameter and 5½ in (13 cm) in height
ice cubes (enough to fill the space between the ready-made candle and the edges of the mold)
approximately 9½ oz (270 g) commercially prepared blue paraffin wax

additional equipment

clear plastic pillar mold, 3¼ in (8 cm) in diameter and 5½ in (13 cm) in height
glass bowl
kitchen towel
rolling pin

PREPARING THE READY-MADE CANDLE: Place the ready-made candle inside the center of the mold. Do not seal the hole in the mold, since it is needed for drainage as the ice melts. Tie the wick of the bought candle to a wooden skewer and rest the skewer across the shoulder of the mold.

PREPARING THE ICE: Stand the mold in a glass bowl that will catch the water as the ice melts. Wrap some ice cubes in a clean cloth and strike them with a rolling pin to crush them. The size of the pieces of crushed ice will determine the appearance of the finished candle; larger pieces will create larger cavities and finer pieces will create smaller, more delicate cavities. Fill the mold to the top with coarsely crushed ice.

PREPARING THE WAX: Place the commercially prepared blue wax in a double boiler and heat it until the wax is molten and reaches a temperature of 210°F (99°C).

FORMING THE CANDLE: Pour the wax carefully down one side of the mold containing the ice and the ready-made candle. Continue pouring until the mold is full. The amount of wax you need will depend on the amount of ice in the mold, so do not be surprised if you have some left over. Simply transfer the excess to a bowl lined with wax paper and allow it to set. The solid wax can then be remelted and used again at a later date.

Set the candle aside for about an hour. As the ice melts the water will pour away through the hole in the bottom of the mold and into the bowl below.

FINISHING: Remove the wick support and slide the candle from the mold. There may be a few pieces of ice that remain inside, but they will soon melt and the water will run off. Allow the candle to stand until completely dry. Trim the revealed wick to about ½ in (1 cm).

tips

Use a clear plastic mold for these candles, since it is exciting to watch the whole process and to see the patterns that the wax and ice form.
Try to ensure that the core candle remains vertical in the center of the mold.

floral embossed

Inexpensive, plastic decorative moldings are used here to create pretty embossed flower patterns on the surface of these citrus-colored, rectangular and square candles.

materials
tracing paper
stiff, shiny cardboard
waterproof glue
2 in (5 cm) diameter wick
10½ oz (300 g) commercially prepared orange paraffin wax

additional equipment
pencil and scissors
ruler
decorative plastic molding, 4 in (10 cm) wide and
    2⅜ in (6 cm) high
double-sided adhesive tape
packing tape

PREPARING THE MOLD: Photocopy the rectangular template on page 77 at 200 percent, then trace and transfer it to stiff cardboard. Cut out the design and score and fold along the dotted lines using a ruler, with the shiny surface facing inward. Glue the decorative plastic molding to one long, shiny side of the mold. Bend the cardboard into shape, then fix the side overlap securely with double-sided adhesive tape. Bend the base flaps under and fix them with double-sided adhesive tape. Wrap the entire mold with packing tape to seal all the joins.

PREPARING THE WICK: Cut two wicks about 2 in (5 cm) longer than the height of the finished candle and prime them (see page 17). Use a wicking needle to pierce two holes through the base of the mold, then thread the wicks through the holes. Tie the wick ends to a wooden skewer and lay the stick across the top of the mold, holding the wicks vertically in the mold. At the base of the mold, pull the wicks taut and seal them with mold sealer. Place the

mold on a cookie sheet and seal around the base with more mold sealer to fix it in place and prevent wax from leaking out.

PREPARING THE WAX: Melt the commercially prepared orange paraffin wax in a double boiler until the wax is molten and reaches a temperature of 180°F (82°C). Pour the wax into the center of the mold, filling it to the top, then set it aside. Keep excess wax for topping it off later. After a few minutes, gently tap the sides of the mold to release any trapped air bubbles. After about an hour, a dip will form around the wicks. Pierce the wax a few times with a cocktail stick, then top it off with wax reheated to 180°F (82°C). Leave it to set completely.

FINISHING: When the wax is cold, remove the mold sealer and slice open the mold with a craft knife to release the candle. Carefully pry the cardboard from the sides so as not to damage the embossed pattern. Remove the wick support and snip off the wicks at the base. Trim the other ends to about ½ in (1 cm).

To make the embossed yellow cube candle, photocopy the cube template on page 77 at 200 percent and stick a 1¼ in (3 cm) square decorative molding with a flower pattern onto the inside of the cardboard mold. Use 9½ oz (270 g) of commercially prepared yellow wax and a single wick.

zen stones

Realistic stone-shaped candles in subtle shades of grey look enchanting when grouped together, perhaps as a centerpiece for a dinner table or as part of a small indoor water feature. A candle mold based on a real pebble can be made using a latex mold-making kit.

materials

1 palm-sized pebble
2 in (5 cm) diameter wick
stiff cardboard
28 oz (800 g) paraffin wax
black pigment
black dye disc
chalky white dye disc
liquid soap
white acrylic paint

additional equipment

small saucer
mold-making kit containing latex mold-making solution
   and thickener
paintbrush
scissors
stencil brush
soft cloth

MAKING THE MOLD: Clean and dry the pebble and place it on an overturned saucer. Following the manufacturer's instructions, apply several coats of the latex mold-making solution to the pebble and the saucer, allowing each coat to dry a little before applying the next one. Aim to build up a layer that is about 1/8 in (3 mm) thick. For the final coat, mix the latex solution with the thickener in a ratio of 20:1, then stir it well. When the mixture has thickened, apply the final coat. Set it aside. When it is completely dry, carefully peel the mold away from the master.

PREPARING THE WICK AND MOLD: Cut an unprimed wick about 2 in (5 cm) longer than the height of the finished candle and thread it through the eye of a wicking needle. Carefully pierce a hole at the base of the mold with the needle, then draw the wick through. Pull the wick taut at the base, leaving about 5/8 in (1.5 cm) revealed, and seal it in place with mold sealer.

Make a support for the rubbery mold using cardboard that is wider than the neck of the water bath. Cut a hole in the center of the cardboard that is just large enough to fit around the shoulder of the mold. Place the mold into the cardboard support, then pass a cocktail stick through the wick. Let the stick lie across the shoulder of the mold, holding the wick vertically in the center of the mold.

PREPARING THE WAX: Place the paraffin wax in a double boiler and heat it to 200°F (93°C). To make a black pebble candle, add a tiny amount of black pigment to the wax. To make a lighter, grey pebble candle, use small portions of black dye disc and add a little chalky white. Cut a small piece off the disc, then crush it roughly with the back of a spoon. Add the crushed dye to the molten wax and stir until it dissolves. The greater the amount of dye used, the stronger the color will be, so start with a small amount and add more later, if required. To get an idea of the approximate finished shade, dip a strip of wax paper into the dyed wax and allow it to dry.

FORMING THE CANDLE: Rest the cardboard support over an empty container and carefully pour the dyed wax into the mold, filling it to the shoulder. Keep excess wax for topping off later. After a few minutes, gently tap the mold to release any trapped air bubbles. Lower the filled mold into a water bath with the cardboard supporting it, and set it aside for an hour. As the wax sets, a dip will form around the wick. Pierce the wax a few times with a cocktail stick. After another hour, top it off with wax reheated to 200°F (93°C). Return the mold to the water bath until the wax is completely set.

FINISHING: Remove the mold from the cardboard support and cover the outside with liquid soap for easy removal. Carefully pull the rubber mold back on itself, releasing the pebble candle. Ease the wick from the base, being careful to not damage the mold. Use a craft knife to trim excess wax and wick from around the base of the candle, leveling off any unevenness so that the candle will stand steadily by itself. Trim the wick to about ½ in (1 cm).

To create a mottled effect, simply stipple a little white acrylic paint onto the candle using a stencil brush. Buff it with a soft cloth after it dries.

To make other stone candles, use different sizes or shapes of pebbles as masters for the mold and vary the colors of the wax for a natural look.

frosted pillars

The popular frosted, scaly appearance of these sturdy pillars is created simply by pouring the wax into the mold at a very low temperature. The wax is stirred while cooling, creating a frothy texture. For a fluffier, lighter look, you could use a wire whisk to whip up the cool wax.

materials
2 in (5 cm) diameter wick
2 oz (60 g) stearin
¼ of a blue dye disc
19 oz (540 g) paraffin wax

additional equipment
clear plastic pillar mold, 2⅜ in (6 cm) in diameter and
    8 in (20 cm) in height
masking tape

PREPARING THE MOLD: This technique involves moving the mold with the wax in it, so you need to use a mold that is taller than the height of the finished candle. Mark the mold with a strip of masking tape 7 in (18 cm) from the base to make the tallest candle.

PREPARING THE WICK: Cut the wick about 2 in (5 cm) longer than the height of the finished candle and prime it (see page 17). Use a wicking needle to thread one end through the hole at the base of the mold. Tie the free end around a wooden skewer and lay the skewer across the top of the mold, holding the wick vertically down the center. At the base of the mold, pull the wick taut and seal it with mold sealer.

PREPARING THE WAX: Melt the stearin in a double boiler. Crush the blue dye with the back of a spoon. Add the dye to the stearin and stir until it dissolves. The greater the amount of dye used, the stronger the color will be, so start with a small amount and add more later, if required. To get an idea of the approximate finished shade, dip a strip of wax paper into the dyed wax and allow it to dry.

Add the paraffin wax and heat it until the wax is molten and reaches a temperature of 180°F (82°C).

THE FROSTING TECHNIQUE: Remove the wax from the heat and allow it to cool, stirring continuously to prevent a skin from forming on the surface. Soon you will see a little scum developing on the surface. When this happens, pour a little wax into the mold. Swirl the wax around the mold to coat the inside up to the mark, then pour the wax back into the pan. Briskly stir the wax again until it becomes frothy. Refill the mold up to the mark and keep excess wax for topping off later. After a few minutes, gently tap the sides of the mold to release any trapped air bubbles. Transfer the candle to a water bath and weigh it down. After about an hour, a dip will form around the wick. Pierce the wax a few times with a cocktail stick, then top off to the marked level with wax that has been reheated and then cooled to a temperature of about 150°F (65°C). Leave it to set completely.

FINISHING: The cold candle will easily slide out of the mold when the sealer is removed. Remove the wick support and snip off the wick so it is level with the base. Trim the revealed end of the wick to about ½ in (1 cm).

Make another frosted pillar in the same way using violet dye. To make the shorter pillars, mark the mold with masking tape 6 in (15 cm) from the base and use 16 oz (450 g) of paraffin wax, 2 oz (50 g) of stearin, and just under ¼ of a dye disc.

tip

The frosting technique causes the finished candle to appear much lighter in color, so remember to take this into consideration when adding your dye disc to the stearin.

additional
embelli

Having mastered the basic techniques of candlemaking, plus a few clever tricks of the trade, you can now try some more adventurous projects that feature the embellishment of simple wax shapes. You can use a host of decorative objects from the home or garden, or purchase items from craft shops. You could even use the information in the following section as a starting point for the creation of themed displays for your home.

Embedding is an important method of embellishment. Essentially, embedding is the insertion of objects, such as shells, glass nuggets, grains, or anything else you can think of, into the outer layer of wax that surrounds the candle. The lustered light and grain-covered pillars use a technique featuring two molds, while the seashell square is formed from "walls" of wax that allow the shells to protrude from the surface.

In addition, wafer-thin, flexible, self-adhesive appliqué wax is available in a vast array of colors, metallic finishes, and holographic effects. The wire effect achieved in the metallic ideas candles shows just a few ways to use this infinitely versatile product. Alternatively, wax glue is a wonderful invention and can be used to firmly attach small decorative objects, such as mirror mosaic tiles, to the surface of a finished candle.

Finally, the recent popularity of aromatherapy has prompted the inclusion of a delightful little collection of fragrant container candles. Deliciously scented, sorbet-colored candles are cast in frosted glass vessels and have both decorative and therapeutic uses.

shments

lustered light

Colorful glass nuggets are often seen at the base of a bowl of water containing floating candles. Here, however, the nuggets are actually embedded within the candle, giving a shimmering luster to a simple square shape.

materials
2 in (5 cm) diameter wick
2 oz (50 g) stearin
16 oz (450 g) paraffin wax
selection of colorful glass nuggets

additional equipment
clear plastic square mold 2⅜ in (6 cm) wide and
    3 in (7.5 cm) high
clear plastic square mold, 3¼ in (8 cm) wide and
    4 in (10 cm) high

PREPARING THE WICK: Cut the wick about 2 in (5 cm) longer than the height of the finished candle and prime it (see page 17). Use a wicking needle to thread one end through the hole at the base of the first mold. Tie the free end around a wooden skewer and lay the skewer across the top of the mold, holding the wick vertically down the center. At the base of the mold, pull the wick taut and seal it with mold sealer.

PREPARING THE WAX: Melt the stearin in a double boiler, then add the paraffin wax. Continue heating the wax until it is molten and reaches a temperature of 180°F (82°C).

FORMING THE CANDLE: Pour as much of the wax as will fit into the center of the mold, filling it to the top. Keep the excess wax for topping off and embedding the nuggets later. After a few minutes, gently tap the mold to release any trapped air bubbles. After about an hour, a dip will form around the wick. Pierce the wax a few times with a cocktail stick, then top it off with wax reheated to 180°F (82°C). Leave it to set completely.

ADDING THE NUGGETS: When the candle is cold, remove the mold sealer and wick support and slide the candle out of the mold. Do not trim the wick yet.

Place the square candle inside the second clear plastic mold. Thread the wick through the hole in the mold and seal it with mold sealer, then attach a wick support to the other end. Position the nuggets between the sides of the two molds to fill the gap. Remelt the remaining paraffin wax in the double boiler. When the mixture has reached 180°F (82°C), pour or spoon it into the gap between the molds, covering the nuggets to a height just above the first candle. Leave it to set.

FINISHING: When the candle is cold, remove the mold sealer and wick support and slide the candle out of the mold. Trim the wick at the base so that the candle stands steadily and snip the revealed end to about ½ in (1 cm).

Use the same technique to make any number of candles using different colored nuggets.

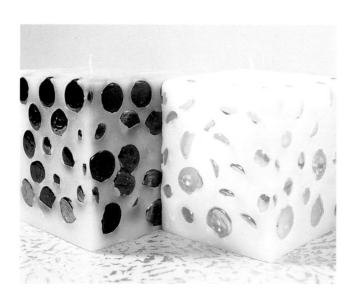

mirror mosaic

In this project, glass mirror tiles are glued around the surface of the candle using special wax glue. This technique can be carried out using a multitude of decorative materials, such as dried flowers and leaves or colorful buttons, for a great range of finished effects. The small, reflective mirror mosaic tiles used here not only create a dazzling display when the candle is used alone but also reflect the warm flickering light from other candles when positioned within a group.

materials
4 in (10 cm) diameter wick and 3 wick sustainers
3½ oz (100 g) stearin
⅕ of a red dye disk
31½ oz (900 g) paraffin wax
selection of mirror mosaic tiles
wax glue

additional equipment
plastic piping (from a building supplier) approximately
    4 in (10 cm) in diameter and 5½ in (14 cm) in height
tile nippers (optional)

PREPARING THE MOLD: Place the plastic piping on some wax paper on a cookie sheet and seal around the base with mold sealer.

PREPARING THE WICKS: Cut three wicks about 2 in (5 cm) longer than the height of the finished candle and prime them (see page 17). Attach one end of each wick to a wick sustainer.

PREPARING THE WAX: Melt the stearin in a double boiler. Crush the red dye with the back of a spoon and add it to the melted stearin, stirring until it dissolves. Dip a strip of wax paper into the dyed stearin to see an approximate finished shade.

Add the paraffin wax to the dyed stearin and continue to heat until the wax is molten and reaches a temperature of 180°F (82°C). Pour a thin layer of wax into the center of the mold. After a few minutes, drop the prepared wicks into the molten wax, evenly spaced apart. Tie the free ends around two wooden skewers and lay the sticks across the top of the mold, holding the wicks vertically.

FORMING THE CANDLE: Reheat the wax to a temperature of 180°F (82°C) and pour it into the center of the mold to fill it. Keep the excess wax for topping off later. After a few minutes, gently tap the sides of the mold to release any trapped air bubbles. After about two hours, a dip will form around the wicks. Pierce the wax a few times with a cocktail stick, then top it off with wax reheated to 180°F (82°C). Leave it to set completely .

RELEASING THE CANDLE: When the wax is completely cold, the candle should easily slide out of the mold when the mold sealer and wick supports are removed. Snip the revealed wick to about ½ in (1 cm).

DECORATING: The mosaic tiles can now be stuck all around the candle using wax glue (follow the manufacturer's instructions). If whole tiles do not fit around the candle accurately, use tile nippers, available from mosaics suppliers, to cut the tiles to size.

To make the lighter candle, use piping approximately 4¾ in (12 cm) in diameter and 4 in (10 cm) in height. Heat 7 oz (200 g) of stearin and 4 lb (1.8 kg) of paraffin wax with approximately ¹⁄₁₀ of a red dye disc.

metallic ideas

The pure frosty whiteness of these sturdy pillars makes them perfect for the winter holiday season, while the metallic decoration only adds to the magic. The silver and gold decoration looks like fine wire, when in fact it is actually very thin strips of flexible, self-adhesive appliqué wax. Simply cut the appliqué wax to size using a ruler and a craft knife and press it into position on the surface of the candle.

materials
2 in (5 cm) diameter wick
2 oz (50 g) stearin
16 oz (450 g) paraffin wax
metallic appliqué wax, 1 sheet per candle

additional equipment
clear plastic pillar mold, 2¾ in (7 cm) in diameter and
7 in (18 cm) in height

PREPARING THE WICK: Cut the wick about 2 in (5 cm) longer than the height of the finished candle and prime it (see page 17). Use a wicking needle to thread one end of the wick through the hole at the base of the mold. Pass a cocktail stick through the wick and rest the stick across the top of the mold, holding the wick vertically down the center. At the base of the mold, pull the wick taut and seal it with mold sealer.

PREPARING THE WAX: Melt the stearin in a double boiler, then add the paraffin wax. Continue to heat until the mixture is molten and reaches a temperature of 180°F (82°C).

FORMING THE CANDLE: Pour the wax into the center of the mold and set it aside. Keep excess wax for topping off later. After a few minutes, gently tap the sides of the mold to release any trapped air bubbles. Place the filled mold in a water bath and weigh it down. After about an hour, a dip will form around the wick. Pierce the wax a few times with a cocktail stick, then top it off with wax reheated to 82°C (180°F). Leave it to set completely.

RELEASING THE CANDLE: The candle will easily slide out of the mold when the mold sealer and wick support are removed. Trim the wick at the base so that the candle stands steadily and snip the revealed end to about ½ in (1 cm).

DECORATING: Metallic appliqué wax comes in preformed sheets of fine strips. It is quite tacky and will adhere to the surface of the candle with only gentle pressure from your fingers. To cover a whole candle, simply wrap the complete sheet around it, either vertically or horizontally, and press down. You may need to trim the sheet slightly with a craft knife to achieve a snug fit. Alternatively, to cover just parts of the candle, cut off the strips with a craft knife and wrap them around the candle individually or in pairs.

To make the shorter candles, use masking tape to mark a height of 6 in (15 cm) from the base of the mold on the outside of the plastic. Use 9½ oz (270 g) of paraffin wax and 1 oz (30 g) of stearin. To make the thinner candle, use a mold that is 2⅜ in (6 cm) in diameter and mark it at a height of about 7 in (18 cm). Use the same amount of wax and stearin as described above.

seashell**square**

This square candle employs a fascinating method of embedding that does
not require a mold. Instead, walls of wax are made so that the decorative tops of
seashells stick out from the wax. Other boldly colored, collected objects may also be used.

materials
selection of seashells, bought from a reputable source
1½ in (4 cm) diameter wick and a wick sustainer
31½ oz (900 g) paraffin wax
wax glue
approximately 3½ oz (100 g) stearin

additional equipment
masking tape
cookie sheet, at least 1 in (2.5 cm) deep and about 12 in
     (30 cm) square (you will be making four 5½ in
     (14 cm) squares, so you can replace one square tray
     with two rectangular trays, if desired)
sharp knife

ARRANGING THE SHELLS: Mark out with masking tape
four 5½ in (14 cm) squares on the cookie sheet, leaving a
small gap between each one. Lay the shells face up in
smaller squares within these marked squares, close to the
bottom line but with a gap of ¾ in (2 cm) on both sides
and 1½ in (4 cm) at the top.

PREPARING THE WICK: Cut the wick about 2 in (5 cm)
longer than the height of the finished candle and prime it
(see page 17). Attach one end to a wick sustainer.

PREPARING THE WAX: The first layer of wax does not
include stearin. Melt the paraffin wax in a double boiler
and continue to heat it until the wax is molten and
reaches a temperature of 180°F (82°C).

THE EMBEDDING TECHNIQUE: Very carefully, pour a thin
layer of wax onto the cookie sheet until it covers half the
height of the shells. Transfer the wax in the boiler to a
bowl lined with wax paper. Leave the wax on the cookie

sheet until it is rubbery but not completely set, then use a
sharp knife to cut out the wax in the originally marked
square shapes, that is, ¾ in (2 cm) on both sides of the
shell square and 1½ in (4 cm) above it. Leave the four
squares of wax to set completely.

FORMING THE CANDLE SHAPE: Fix the corners of the
four wax "walls" together using wax glue, following the
manufacturer's instructions. Place this empty wax mold
on some wax paper on a cookie sheet.

FORMING THE CANDLE: Weigh out the remaining wax
and calculate how much stearin you now need (10 percent
stearin to 90 percent wax). Heat the stearin in the double
boiler until molten, then add the paraffin wax. Reheat until
molten and reaches a temperature of 180°F (82°C). Pour a
thin layer into the center of the wax box, to where the shell
square begins. After a few minutes, drop the prepared
wick into the molten wax in the center of the mold. Tie the
free end around a wooden skewer and lay it across the top
of the mold, holding the wick vertically down the center.

FORMING THE CANDLE: Let the remaining wax cool to a
temperature no greater than 150°F (65°C). It is important
that the refill wax is not too hot, or it will melt the
embedded wax. Pour the cooled wax back into the mold
in about four layers, letting the surface of each layer
become rubbery before adding the next. After the final
layer, keep the excess wax for topping off later. After
about two hours, a dip will form around the wick. Pierce
the wax a few times with a cocktail stick, then top off with
wax cooled to 150°F (65°C). Leave it to set completely.

FINISHING: When the wax is completely cold, remove
the wick support and snip the wick to ½ in (1 cm).

grain-covered pillars

Raid your kitchen cupboards for different colored grains to use in this project. Green pumpkin seeds, red adzuki beans, and yellow and beige wheat grains are used here, but you could try orange lentils and yellow split peas, which blend wonderfully with neutral and wild rice mixtures. You can also use small beads as a substitute for grains.

materials
2 in (5 cm) diameter wick
2 oz (60 g) stearin
19 oz (540 g) paraffin wax
selection of grains (pumpkin seeds
    are used here)

additional equipment
clear plastic pillar mold, 2⅜ in (6 cm)
    in diameter and 7 in (18 cm)
    in height
clear plastic pillar mold 2¾ in (7 cm)
    in diameter and 8 in (20 cm)
    in height

PREPARING THE WICK: Cut the wick about 2 in (5 cm) longer than the height of the finished candle and prime it (see page 17). Use a wicking needle to thread one end of the wick through the hole at the base of the first mold. Tie the free end around a wooden skewer and lay the skewer across the top of the mold, holding the wick vertically down the center. At the base of the mold, pull the wick taut and seal it with mold sealer.

PREPARING THE WAX: Melt the stearin in a double boiler, then add the paraffin wax. Continue heating the wax until it is molten and reaches a temperature of 180°F (82°C).

FORMING THE CANDLE: Pour as much of the wax as will fit into the center of the mold, filling it to the top. Keep the excess wax for topping off and grain embellishment later. After a few minutes, gently tap the mold to release any trapped air bubbles. After about an hour, a dip will form around the wick. Pierce the wax a few times with a cocktail stick, then top it off with wax reheated to 180°F (82°C). Leave it to set completely.

ADDING THE GRAINS: When the candle is cold, remove the mold sealer and wick support and slide the candle out of the mold. Do not trim the wick yet.

Place the pillar candle inside the second plastic mold. Thread the wick through the hole in the mold and seal it with mold sealer, then attach a wick support to the other end. Pour pumpkin seeds between the sides of the two molds to fill the gap. Remelt the remaining paraffin wax in the double boiler. When the mixture has reached 180°F (82°C), pour or spoon it into the gap between the molds, covering the seeds to a height just above the first candle. Leave it to set.

FINISHING: When the wax is cold, the grain-covered candle will easily slide out of the mold when the mold sealer and wick support are removed. Trim the wick at the base so that the candle stands steadily and snip the revealed end to about ½ in (1 cm).

To make the red candle, use a first mold that is 1½ in (4 cm) in diameter and 4¾ in (12 cm) in height and a total of 16 oz (270 g) of paraffin wax and 1 oz (30 g) of stearin. Fill the mold to a height of approximately 3¼ in (8 cm). Place the finished candle in a mold that measures 2 in (5 cm) in diameter and 5½ in (14 cm) in height, and fill the gap with red adzuki beans and reheated wax. Use the same molds to make a yellow candle embellished with beige and yellow wheat grains. Fill the first mold to a height of 4¾ in (12 cm) and use 19 oz (540 g) of paraffin wax and 2 oz (60 g) of stearin.

essential scents

These small, tapered, frosted glass containers hold delicious sorbet-colored candles scented with fragrant essential oils. Aromatherapy is an ancient holistic practice, the benefits of which are being rediscovered and enjoyed by many people today. Use the essential oils suggested on the next page, which have been selected for their relaxing, sensual, calming, and uplifting properties. Or mix your own special blend to match your mood. A large selection is available at health food stores.

materials
2 in (5 cm) diameter wick and a wick sustainer
½ oz (15 g) stearin
approximately ¹⁄₁₂ of a violet dye disc
5½ oz (150 g) paraffin wax
essential oil

additional equipment
tapered, frosted square glass jar, 2⅜ in (6 cm) wide at the
    base and 2⅜ in (6 cm) tall

PREPARING THE WICK: Cut the wick about 2 in (5 cm) longer than the height of the glass container and prime it (see page 17). Attach one end to a wick sustainer and drop the wick into the glass jar. Pass a cocktail stick through the wick and rest it across the top of the mold, holding the wick vertically down the center.

tip

When using glass containers, it is important to remember to center the wick. If the candle flame touches the glass, the container will crack or break.

PREPARING THE WAX: Melt the stearin in a double boiler. Crush the violet dye with the back of a spoon. You only need this very small amount of dye to achieve a pale, delicate color. Add the dye to the stearin and stir until it dissolves. To get an idea of the approximate finished shade, dip a strip of wax paper into the dyed stearin and allow it to dry.

Add the paraffin wax and heat it until the wax is molten and reaches a temperature of 180°F (82°C). Add a few drops of essential oil. The amount you add will depend on your own personal taste, but remember that essential oils are concentrated and only a few drops are usually required. Completely blend the oil into the wax.

FORMING THE CANDLE: Pour the wax into the center of the glass mold and keep the excess wax for topping off later. After a few minutes, gently tap the sides of the mold to release any trapped air bubbles that will distort the finished candle. After about an hour, a dip will form around the wick. Pierce the wax a few times around the wick with a cocktail stick, then top it off with wax reheated to 180°F (82°C), taking care not to fill it above the original level of wax. Put the candle aside to set completely.

FINISHING: Remove the wick support, then trim the wick to about ½ in (1 cm).

Repeat the same process to make more candles, using small amounts of pink, yellow, and orange dye discs to create similar sorbet colors. Use different fragrances individually or blended together.

properties of essential oils

CITRONELLA	**CHAMOMILE**	**LAVENDER**	**YLANG YLANG**	**ROSE**
In addition to its revitalizing citrus aroma, citronella essential oil has insect repellent qualities ideal for balmy summer evenings spent outdoors.	Chamomile essential oil has a distinctive smell, much like that of overripe apples, and is well-known for its calming and tranquillizing properties.	Lavender is a familiar fragrance to many people, and the essential oil is traditionally regarded as reviving yet soothing. It also has antiseptic qualities.	Sensual ylang ylang essential oil is reputed to be an aphrodisiac and an antidepressant. In Indonesia, ylang ylang flowers are spread on the bed of newlyweds on their wedding night.	Rose essential oil is great for calming anger, anxiety, and mental tension, as well as for regulating mood swings caused by premenstrual syndrome.

troubleshooting guide

If you carefully follow the instructions given for each project and abide by the safety guidelines, your candlemaking experience should be pleasurable and hazard free. The resulting candles should burn beautifully, evenly, and without excess smoke or sputtering. However, here are a few common problems and suggestions for how you should deal with them.

CLEANING UP: It is a good idea to cover your work surfaces and the surrounding area with newspaper, to protect against wax spills. However, in the event of a spill onto an unprotected surface, don't panic. Simply leave the wax to cool, then pick or scrape it off. If it falls on fabric or upholstery, pick off as much cool wax as you can, then place brown paper over the stain and press it with a hot iron. The wax will remelt and be absorbed by the paper. However, dark colors and powder dyes may leave a stain on the surface once the wax is removed.

DYES: Use powder dye sparingly, since the color is very concentrated, and add only a tiny speck at a time. You can always add more, but you can't take it away.

HOT WAX: Candlemaking is a relatively safe craft, but great care must be taken to avoid accidents when using a heat source. Never leave a double boiler unattended, as the wax can ignite when it is heated to too high a temperature. If the wax begins to smoke, it is in danger of ignition. If it does ignite, turn off the heat immediately and smother the flames with a damp towel or a saucepan lid. Do not try to extinguish the flames with water.

When pouring wax, always take care to avoid splashes. It is a good idea to wear protective gloves.

MOLDS: Ready-made molds must be washed in hot, soapy water immediately after use. Any wax left in the mold will spoil the surface of the next candle to be cast.

When using cardboard molds, carefully seal all joins with packing tape to prevent seepage. Place the mold on a cookie sheet, so that wax that does leak will be caught. Seepage may not harm the finished candle, but if a lot of wax has leaked out before the candle has set, there is nothing more to do other than to save the wax for remelting.

RELEASING THE CANDLE: If you cannot remove the candle from the mold, there may have been too little stearin in the wax mixture. This means that the candle set too slowly, causing insufficient contraction. Place the mold in the refrigerator for a while, then try again. If the wax was topped off above the original level, a little of it may have seeped between the candle and the mold, making removal difficult. Place the mold in very hot water for a short while, and then try again.

WAX TEMPERATURE: Correct temperature is the key element in successful candlemaking. Use a special wax thermometer or a sugar thermometer to monitor the molten wax regularly, and pour the wax into the mold at the temperature indicated for each project.

For the frosted effect, it is necessary for the wax to be cooled before pouring; the scaly appearance will not work with wax that is too hot. Set the molten wax to the side and constantly monitor its temperature with the thermometer as it cools. Pour it into the mold at the temperature specified in the project's instructions.

When making striped candles, remember to allow each layer to cool just until the surface becomes rubbery enough to support the next layer, but not so cool as to cause separation, or so hot as to cause loss of definition.

WICKS: To ensure even burning, the wick should be matched as closely as possible to the diameter of the candle. If a wick is too thick, the candle will supply insufficient fuel and the wick will burn with a large flame, producing unpleasant smoke. If the wick is too thin, it will drown in the molten wax and the flame will be extinguished, or else the flame will be very small.

Another important point to remember is that the wick should be centrally placed; an off-center wick will produce lopsided burning.

templates

The following templates need to be enlarged to their correct size.
To do this, photocopy each one at the percentage specified below.

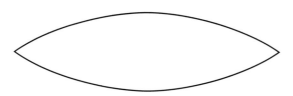

Slim jims (see page 28) photocopy at 200 percent

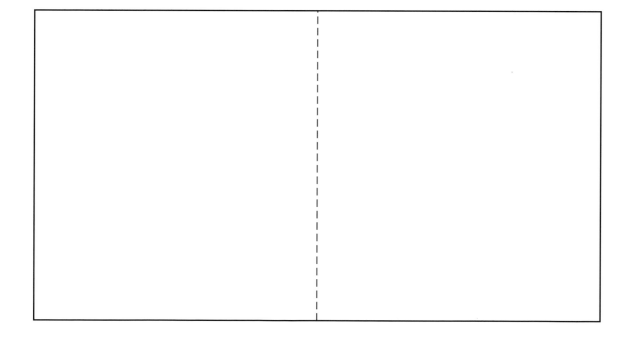

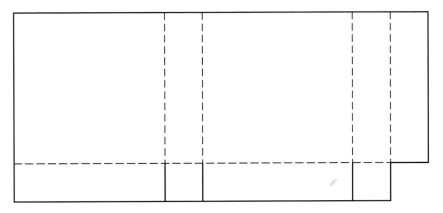

Rothko-esque (see page 50) photocopy at 400 percent (you will need two sheets of 11 x 17 or A3 paper)

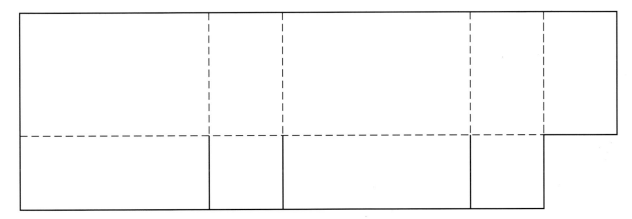

Floral embossed, rectangle (see page 54) photocopy at 200 percent

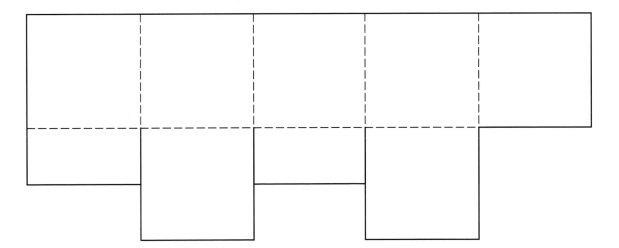

Floral embossed, square (see page 55) photocopy at 200 percent

list of suppliers

There are many craft suppliers who sell candlemaking materials. Try to find the ones in your area, since wax is heavy and costly to ship. There are also mail-order suppliers who carry a more complete or specialized line of candlemaking materials.

CANDLEMAKING SUPPLIES:

Barker Candle Supplies
15106 10th Avenue SW
Seattle, WA 98166
(800) 543-0601
www.barkerco.com

Betterbee Inc.
8 Meader Road
Greenwich, NY 12834
(518) 692-9669
(800) 632-3379

The Candlemaker
5626 Broad Street
Greendale, WI 53129
(414) 423-5399
(888) 251-4618
www.thecandlemaker.com

The Candlewic Company
8244 Easton Road
Ottsville, PA 18942
(610) 847-2076
www.candlewic.com

Dadant and Sons, Inc.
51 South Second Street
Hamilton, IL 62341
(217) 847-3324
(800) 637-7464
www.dadant.com

Dick Blick
PO Box 1267
Galesburg, IL 61402
(800) 447-8192
www.dickblick.com

Earth Guild
33 Haywood Street
Asheville, NC 28801
(800) 327-8448
www.earthguild.com

Georgie's Ceramic and Clay Co.
756 NE Lombard
Portland, OR 97211
(503) 283-1353
(800) 999-2529
www.georgies.com

Glorybee
PO Box 2744
Eugene, OR 97402
(541) 689-0913
(800) GLORYBE
www.glorybee.com

Honey Wax
501 South 1st Street
Hackensack, MN 56452-2001
(800) 880-7694, ext. 101
www.mannlakeltd.com

Knorr Beeswax Products, Inc.
1965 Kellogg Avenue
Carlsbad, CA 92008
(760) 431-2007
(800) 807-BEES

Lapp's Bee Supply Center
500 South Main Street
PO Box 460
Reeseville, WI 53579
(800) 321-1960

Pourette
1418 NW 53rd Street
PO Box 70469
Seattle, WA 98107
(206) 789-3188
(800) 888-WICK (9425)
www.pourette.com

Spore Handicrafts Inc.
12195 US 12 West
White Pigeon, MI 49099
(616) 483-9631

Walnut Hill Candlemaking Supplies
Green Lane and Wilson Avenue
PO Box 599
Bristol, PA 19007
(215) 785-6511
(800) NEED WAX

COLOR AND SCENT SUPPLIES:

French Color and Chemical Co.
488 Grand Avenue
Englewood, NJ 07631
(201) 567-6883
(800) 762-9098
www.frenchcolor.com

J&E Polish Co.
146 Court Street
Brockton, MA 02302
(508) 587-9400

SCENT SUPPLIES:

The Essential Oil Company
1719 SE Umatilla Street
Portland, OR 97202
(503) 872-8772
(800) 729-5912
www.essentialoil.com

The Lebermuth Co. Inc.
PO Box 4103
South Bend, IN 46634-4103
(219) 259-7000
(800) 648-1123
www.lebermuth.com

The Rosemary House
120 South Market Street
Mechanicsburg, PA 17055
(717) 697-5111

Uncommon Scents
380 West 1st Avenue
Eugene, OR 97401
(800) 426-4336
www.uncommonscents.com

CHEMICAL SUPPLIES:

Chem Lab Supplies
1060 Ortega Way, Unit C
Placentia, CA 92670
(714) 630-7902
www.chemlab.com

MOLD SUPPLIES:

Clay Art Center
2636 Pioneer Way East
Tacoma, WA 98404
(206) 922-5342
(800) 952-8030
www.clayartcenter.com

North Valley Candle Molds
6928 Danyeur Road
Redding, CA 96001
(530) 247-0447
(877) 818-6653
www.moldman.com

Smooth-On Products
(call for distributor near you)
(800) 762-0744
(800) 766-6841

WAX SUPPLIES:

Consult the *Yellow Pages* under
"Wax" or "Petroleum Products."

Aldert Chemicals Ltd.
4889 Dundas Street W., Suite 5
Islington, ON M9A 1B2
(416) 236-4222
www.accessv.com/~aldert

Aztex Enterprises
PO Box 50070
Knoxville, TN 37950
(615) 588-5357
(800) 369-5357
www.aztexonline.com

Dussek Campbell Inc.
3650 Touhy Avenue
PO Box 549
Skokie, IL 60076
(847) 679-6300
(800) 628-9299
www.dussekwax.com

Dussek Campbell
145 Sylvester Road
South San Francisco, CA 94080
(415) 583-3270
(800) 828-9299
www.dussekwax.com

The International Group (IGI)
85 Old Eagle School Road
PO Box 384
Wayne, PA 19087
(610) 687-9030
(800) 852-6537
www.igiwax.com

Reed Wax
167 Pleasant Street
PO Box 508
Reading, MA 01867-0690
(781) 944-4640
(800) 336-5877

WAX-MELTING SYSTEMS:

The D.C. Cooper Corp.
PO Box 210
Jct. 116/94
Stronghurst, IL 61480
(309) 924-1941

Waage Electric Inc.
720 Colfax Avenue
PO Box 337
Kenilworth, NJ 07033
(908) 245-9363
(800) 922-4365
www.waage.com

Other Storey Titles You Will Enjoy

The Candlemaker's Companion,
Betty Oppenheimer,
Storey Books, 1997.
ISBN 0-88266-994-X.

The Handmade Book,
Angela James,
Storey Books, 2000.
ISBN 1-58017-256-3.

The Handmade Paper Book,
Angela Ramsay,
Storey Books, 1999.
ISBN 1-58017-174-5.

The Soapmaker's Companion,
Susan Miller Cavitch,
Storey Books, 1997.
ISBN 0-88266-994-X.

These and other Storey books are
available at your bookstore, farm
store, garden center, or directly
from Storey Books, Schoolhouse
Road, Pownal, Vermont 05261,
or by calling 1-800-441-5700.
Or visit our Web site at
www.storeybooks.com